KU-718-219

PENGUIN BOOKS

Freedom, Fame, Lying
and Betrayal

Leszek Kołakowski was born in 1927 in Radom, Poland. He studied at Łodz University for the period 1945–50 and then at Warsaw University, where he took his D. Phil. in 1953. At Warsaw he was made Assistant Professor and then, in 1959, Chairman and, in 1964, Professor of the Section of the History of Philosophy. For a number of years during the same period he worked in the Institute of Philosophy of the Polish Academy of Sciences. He was also sometime editor-in-chief of the main philosophical journal in Poland and other journals. Having been expelled from his university post by the Polish government in March 1968 for political reasons, he became Visiting Professor in the Department of Philosophy at McGill University, Montreal, for the period 1968–9, and then, during 1969–70, in the Department of Philosophy at the University of California, Berkeley. In 1975 he served as Visiting Professor in the Department of Philosophy at Yale University. From 1981 to 1994 he was Professor on the Committee of Social Thought at the University of Chicago. He was a Senior Research Fellow of All Souls College Oxford from 1970 until his retirement in 1995.

Leszek Kołakowski is the author of over thirty books. Those written in or translated into English include *Main Current of Marxism* (3 vols. 1978); *Religion* (1982); *Bergson* (1984); *Husserl and the Search for Certitude* (1976); *Metaphysical Horror* (1988), *Presence of Myth* (1989); *Modernity on Endless Trial* (1995); and *God Owes Us Nothing: A Brief Remark on Pascal's Religion and the Spirit of Jansenism* (1995). He has written books in Polish, French and German and translated philosophical texts into many different langauges, and has also written three books of a literary character.

He is a Fellow of the British Academy, the Académie Universelle des Cultures, Academia Europa and the Bayerische Akademie der Künste; a Foreign Fellow of the American Academy of Arts and Sciences; and a member of the International Institute of Philosophy, the PEN Club, and of philosophical associations in Britain and Poland.

He has been widely honoured, and has received the Jurzykowski Prize, 1969; Friedenpreis des Deutschen Buchhandels, 1977; Prix Européen d'Essai, 1981; Praemium Erasmianum, 1982; McArthur Fellowship, 1983; Jefferson Award, 1956; Prix Tocqueville, 1993; Premio Nonino, 1997; Prize of Polish PEN Club 1988; and six doctorates *honoris causa*.

FREEDOM, FAME, LYING AND BETRAYAL

Essays on Everyday Life

LESZEK KOŁAKOWSKI

Translated by
Agnieszka Kołakowska

PENGUIN BOOKS

PENGUIN BOOKS

Published by the Penguin Group
Penguin Books Ltd, 27 Wrights Lane, London W8 5TZ, England
Penguin Putnam Inc., 375 Hudson Street, New York, New York 10014, USA
Penguin Books Australia Ltd, Ringwood, Victoria, Australia
Penguin Books Canada Ltd, 10 Alcorn Avenue, Toronto, Ontario, Canada M4V 3B2
Penguin Books (NZ) Ltd, Private Bag 102902, NSMC, Auckland, New Zealand

Penguin Books Ltd, Registered Offices: Harmondsworth, Middlesex, England

First published in Penguin Books 1999
1 3 5 7 9 10 8 6 4 2

Copyright © Leszek Kołakowski, 1999
Translation copyright © Agnieszka Kołakowska, 1999

All rights reserved

The moral right of the author and translator has been asserted

Typeset in Monotype Century Schoolbook
Typeset by Rowland Phototypesetting Ltd, Bury St Edmunds, Suffolk
Printed in England by Clays Ltd, St Ives plc

Except in the United States of America, this book is sold subject
to the condition that it shall not, by way of trade or otherwise, be lent,
re-sold, hired out, or otherwise circulated without the publisher's
prior consent in any form of binding or cover other than that in
which it is published and without a similar condition including this
condition being imposed on the subsequent purchaser

CONTENTS

1
ON POWER

A former British Chancellor of the Exchequer, when asked in a television interview whether he would like to be Prime Minister, replied, with some surprise, that surely everyone would like to be Prime Minister. This was, in turn, a matter of some astonishment to me, for I am by no means convinced that everyone would like to be Prime Minister; on the contrary, I am sure that there are a great many people who have never harboured such a dream, not because they feel that their chances of fulfilling such an ambition are slim, but simply because they think it must be a dreadful kind of job to have to do: endless headaches, huge responsibilities, and the knowledge that whatever you do you will be a permanent target of attacks and ridicule, and the worst intentions will be imputed to you.

Is it true, then, that 'everyone wants power'? The answer depends on how broadly we understand the term. In its broadest sense, 'power' is everything that allows us to influence our surroundings, human or natural, in a desired direction; when we have done this, we are said to have 'mastered' them. When a child takes its first steps, or stands up by itself for the first time, it gains a degree of power over its own body, and is visibly pleased by this; and in general it would be true to say that we would all prefer to have more rather than less mastery over our bodies and those parts of them, like muscles and joints, which can be controlled. Similarly, when we learn a new language, or chess, or swimming, or a branch of mathematics that is new to us, we are acquiring skills whereby we are able to 'master' a new area of culture.

Such a broad understanding of 'power' has been the basis of theories concluding that all human activity is inspired by the desire for power in its various forms; according to such theories, all our efforts are nothing but expressions of a striving for power, the wellspring of human energy. People seek wealth because wealth gives them power not only over things but also to a certain (often considerable) extent over other people. Even sex may be explained in terms of power: either we want to possess the other person's body, and through it the actual person, or we think that by possessing it we are excluding others from possession; either way we have the satisfaction of feeling that we are wielding power over somone. Sex is of course one of nature's pre-human inventions; and according to such theories the desire for power is an instinct present throughout the natural world, whatever the culturally influenced forms it may assume in human society.

It is even possible, with a bit of effort, to explain acts of altruism in terms of power: when we act kindly towards other people, we are motivated, whether we know it or not, by a desire to exercise a measure of control over their lives, for our act of kindness puts them partially in our power. There is no area of our lives that is not motivated by the search for power; there is nothing else, and to say otherwise is self-deception. So the theory goes.

Theories of this type, while they have a superficial plausibility, in fact explain very little. Any theory that attempts to explain all human behaviour in terms of a single type of motivation, or claims that all social life is inspired by a single motivating force, can be defended. This very fact, however, shows that all such theories are in the end no more than philosophical constructs, and therefore of little use. To say, for example, that a person's motives are the same whether he sacrifices himself for his fellow-man or tortures him, does not get us very far forward, for it amounts to saying that there are no valid principles whereby we might judge or indeed even distinguish between such actions: their essence, however different it may seem, is exactly the same. Such theories do, however, have their uses: wrongs committed will not weigh quite so heavily on one's conscience if one can say to oneself that everyone else, at heart, is just as bad.

Certain currents in Christian thought, once powerful although all but obsolete today, could lead us to a similar kind of temptation: if we are told that without divine grace we shall always do evil, whatever we do, while with it we shall necessarily do only good, then it matters little whether we help our fellow man or torture him; without divine grace we shall be banished to hell either way. This has been the fate of all pagans, however noble.

Proponents of such theories always search for a single master-key which could open all doors. But there is no such thing as one satisfactory explanation for everything, and there is no such key. Culture develops and grows because people are inspired by different things and motivated by new needs; old needs shed their dependence on their previous functions and become autonomous parts of the culture.

While theories claiming that all our actions are inspired essentially by a desire for power are naive and of little explanatory value, it is nevertheless true that power itself remains a good that is highly sought-after. When we talk about power we generally intend it in a narrower sense than the one we have been discussing: as the means available to an individual or a collective entity to influence others and control their behaviour, by force or by the threat of force. Power in this sense requires some organized means of coercion, and nowadays this means a state.

Is it true that we all want power in this sense? Certainly, we would all like other people to behave in ways we deem appropriate, which is to say in ways that are beneficial to us, or in accordance with our own sense of justice. It does not follow from this, however, that we would all like to be king. As Pascal said, only a king deprived of his throne is unhappy because he is not king.

We know that power corrupts – not always, but often enough. We also know that people who have enjoyed a substantial measure of power for a significant amount of time often come to feel that they have some kind of natural right to it, just as monarchs once believed that they ruled by divine right. When such people lose their power for one reason or another, they see their loss not merely as a misfortune but as a castastrophe of cosmic proportions. Finally, we know that the struggle for power has been the principal source of wars and other ills that beset the world.

The existence of all these evils connected with power has naturally given rise to a variety of childish anarchist utopias, according to which the only cure for the world's ills is to eliminate power altogether. In the more extreme of these, 'power' is understood in its broadest sense, so that, for instance, the power of parents over their children is considered by its very nature to be a horrible tyranny, to be abolished as soon as possible. It follows that when we teach our children their native language, for example, we are actually exercising a dreadful kind of tyranny: by virtue of the power we wield over them, we are imposing our wishes on them by force, and depriving them of their liberty. It would be best, according to such theories, to leave them in an animal state in which they could invent their own language, customs and culture.

Less absurd varieties of anarchism, however, aim to abolish only political power; the theory is that if all governments, administrations and courts were to disappear, humanity would live in a natural state of peace and brotherhood. Fortunately, it is not possible to bring about an anarchist revolution whenever one feels like it, merely by deciding to do so: anarchy comes about only when all organs and institutions of power collapse and there is no one left in control. The results of such a situation are inevitable: some force which seeks absolute power for itself (and there is no lack of such) will profit from the general mayhem to impose its own despotic order. The most spectacular example of this was of course the Russian Revolution, when a despotic bolshevik regime took power as a result of general anarchy. In practice, anarchy is the handmaiden of tyranny.

Power cannot be abolished, it can only be made better or worse by substituting one sort of government for another. Nor, unfortunately, is it true that we would all live in peaceful brotherhood if only political power were abolished. It is not accident but human nature itself that makes our interests diverge and conflict; there is a measure of aggression in us all, and there is no limit to our needs and desires. It is fairly plain, therefore, that if the institutions of political power were miraculously to vanish, the result would be not universal brotherhood but universal slaughter.

There has never been, nor will there be, a 'government of the people' in the literal sense; apart from anything else, it would not be technically feasible. There can only be certain safeguards whereby the people can keep an eye on what the government is doing and replace it with another if it so chooses. Of course, once a government is in power, we are subject to a variety of restraints, and in a number of important areas the choices are not ours to make: we cannot choose, for example, whether or not to send our children to school, pay our taxes, take a driving test if we wish to drive, and so on. The controls set up by a people to oversee its government are not infallible; a democratically elected government can also be corrupt, and its decisions often contrary to the wishes of the majority; no government can satisfy everyone; and so on. All these are things we know very well. The means by which a people exercises control over its government are never perfect, but the most effective way mankind has so far invented to avoid tyranny is precisely to go on strengthening the instruments of social control over governments and restricting the range of government powers to the bare minimum necessary to maintain social order: the regulation of all areas of our lives, after all, is what totalitarian power is all about.

We may, then, and indeed we should, treat the organs of political power with suspicion, control them closely and if need be (and the need is always there) complain about them; we should not, however, complain of the very existence of power and its institutions, unless we can invent a different world – something many have tried, but none successfully.

2
ON FAME

Fame, we all know, is among the things people most desire. This is so obviously true that there is no need to go into why it should be so — why fame is so famously desirable. It is enough to say that to be famous, for whatever reason, is to affirm oneself and confirm one's own existence, and self-affirmation seems to be a natural human need.

The thirst for fame, however, is not universal, in spite of the fact that in our own civilization fame is a goal obsessively pursued. Some ancient philosophers (famous ones, naturally), especially the Stoics and the Epicureans, even taught that fame was something to be avoided, and advised us to live in hiding and count the blessings of being unknown. Fame doubtless does have its bothersome aspects, although the famous people who complain of its being a terrible burden to them generally lack credibility, because at the same time they do their best to get themselves on television and their names into the newspapers. There are many people, however, who genuinely do not seek fame – either because they lack confidence and do not like being in the limelight, or perhaps because they have a low opinion of themselves.

Fame, as we know, often – but not always – brings wealth. It brings wealth to people in certain professions: actors and film directors, rock singers, sportsmen, and so on. Most people who seek fame, however, do so not for the benefits it brings but for its own sake – mindful, perhaps, of the immortal example of Herostrates, who is said to have burnt down the temple of Diana for the sole reason that he wanted to achieve fame (a purpose in which, it must be said, he succeeded admirably, for here we are still talking about him centuries later). Even today we see loutish youths, barely in their teens, committing hideous crimes of the kind they see on television with the sole aim of becoming famous. At the other end of the scale there are people who already possess the things that sometimes result from fame, such as great wealth, and yet prefer to avoid fame itself and remain unknown. In general, however, fame is considered desirable in itself, and not merely as a means of obtaining other desirable goods.

Fame, by its very nature, is given to few: its rarity is part of its definition. It has been said (by Andy Warhol, who was famous) that one day we shall all have our fifteen minutes of fame; this, however, is nonsense. It is nonsense for two reasons: first, because a simple calculation will show that the process of giving each one of us his fifteen minutes of fame, perhaps on some kind of international television channel, would take, given the current world population, something in the region of 200,000 years, even if that channel broadcast around the clock and showed nothing but successive aspirants to their fifteen minutes of fame, and was watched around the clock by the entire population of the world; and second, because in a situation of such absurd equality no one would be famous at all. Fame must be rare, and this is why it is inevitable that only a very few of those who dream of fame will see their dream fulfilled, and most will be bitterly disillusioned. They will have wasted much time and effort, for making the achievement of fame one's life's goal is a time-consuming business. There are, of course, many goods that people seek but rarely attain, and yet think worth the effort of seeking in spite of the improbability of attaining them. Millions of people, for instance, play the lottery, even though they know that their chances of winning the jackpot are slim. But playing the lottery is cheap (unless it is done compulsively) and involves little time or effort, while aspiring to fame involves a great deal, usually wasted.

There are many degrees of fame, so many that it is impossible to determine precisely who is really famous and who is not. If we disregard those who are famous by virtue of their office, like presidents and prime ministers of world powers, kings and popes, we can say that nowadays fame is usually proportionate to the length and frequency of people's appearances on film and television. In America everyone knows the names and faces of newsreaders and popular television show hosts. We can all recognize Jack Nicholson and (more recently) Emma Thompson; we have all heard of Antonioni and Wajda. We know the names of some scientists from the first half of the century, like Einstein, Planck, Bohr or Marie Curie-Sklodowska; but how many of us who are not chemists or physicists could name the Nobel Prize laureates of the last forty years in physics or chemistry? We do not know their names; sometimes we do not even know how they have distinguished themselves, or in exactly what field. We just assume that they must be illustrious and distinguished. But they are not famous, because so few of us have heard of them.

Reflections of this kind can give rise to the silly supposition that fame is somehow 'unjustly' distributed. The supposition is silly because we do not know what a 'just' distribution of fame would look like, nor how we should go about organizing such a distribution. It is true that, as things are, some barely literate boxing champion can be famous throughout the world while a great scholar or scientist who genuinely works for the benefit of mankind, a medical researcher, say, is known only to a handful of people; but why should there be anything wrong in this? Why *should* fame be the just reward for great intellectual achievements but not for feats of sportsmanship or for hosting a television show? Fame is often a question of sheer luck: even a lottery winner can be famous for a short time, through no effort or merit of his own. Quite often, too, we ourselves, as an audience, can make someone famous: we can establish the fame of an actress, for example, by going to see the films in which she is playing. Many people – Xanthippe, Theo van Gogh, Pontius Pilate – acquire fame simply because they are in some way connected with famous people. And why should they not? There is no sense in complaining about the 'unjust' distribution of fame, for fame is not, and is not supposed to be, a reward for goodness, wisdom, courage or any other virtue; it simply isn't, and it never will be.

This is all to the good. For if our lives were not in large degree unpredictable and governed by chance, they would be very boring indeed, and this in spite of the fact that chance generally does not act in our favour. The universe is not arranged on a basis of just rewards, and we cannot even conceive of what it would mean to say that it could be arranged differently from the way in which it is. Perhaps in heaven fame and glory are awarded according to different rules; perhaps there the famous, those who are elevated to the highest level, will be people no one on earth has heard of. It is safe to assume, however, that those who feverishly pursue fame on earth, consumed with envy at the sight of others whom chance has made famous, will not be among them. The desperate hordes of would-be Nobel Prize winners and would-be American presidents, all seething with resentment at being denied a reward they have so clearly earned, should not seek comfort in the thought that heaven will reward them for their pains. For indeed it is unlikely that God will clothe us in glory as a reward for our envy and vanity.

The thirst for fame and the feeling of injustice at not having it, or not as much as one deserves, is of course the result of vanity, and has nothing to do with intelligence. Moralists have known for centuries that our intellect is powerless in the face of our own vanity and conceit. We have probably all come across otherwise quite intelligent people who are nevertheless shunned like the plague because they are pompous, self-important and smug; the kind of people who burden us with lectures and un-wanted advice and, when we flee their company, either pretend not to notice or attribute it to their great moral and intellectual superiority. We all know perfectly intel-ligent people who constantly complain that no one appre-ciates them, despite their great wisdom and foresight, and refuse to see how ridiculous they sound. Others make themselves into martyrs and constantly demand our sympathy, although given the events of our age their martyrdom is of a rather modest kind; they, too, refuse to see how ridiculous they sound. There are some perfectly intelligent men who make it clear to us at every opportunity that all the women in the world have but one desire, namely to go to bed with them. The intellect cannot conquer vanity. Nor is it an accident that the word 'vanity' is close to 'void'.

The pursuit of fame need not, however, be contemptible or unworthy if two conditions are fulfilled. First, it must be incidental to the main goal, which should be the achievement of something worthwhile for its own sake; that is where our efforts should be concentrated, even if we are also tempted by the prospect of the fame that may accrue to us as a result. Secondly, the pursuit of fame should not be allowed to turn into an obsession, for this, in addition to being almost always futile, may generate a destructive feeling of resentment against the world which can ruin one's life. On the whole it is better not to think of fame at all, but to be content with the affection and respect of even a small circle of family and good friends.

3

ON EQUALITY

Let us consider the meaning of the statement, once revolutionary and now merely banal, that 'all men are equal'. It is not an injunction: it does not mean that everyone *should* be treated equally in the eyes of the law. If it did, one could argue that such an injunction is itself arbitrary, for why, after all, *should* the law treat everyone equally? Rather, the injunction follows from the descriptive statement that all men *are* equal, and for this reason the law should be the same for all. Thus the injunction is grounded in a certain state of affairs which obtains in fact. But what is this state of affairs, and how can we know that it really does obtain?

Some people try to deny the truth of the statement that all men are equal by pointing out that we all differ in so many ways – in our abilities, our knowledge, our natures, and so on – that we cannot possibly be equal; but they are mistaken. For we all know that people are not identical, and differ in a variety of ways; and those who proclaim equality as a fact, a state of affairs that is independent of those differences, also know it. It therefore makes no sense to deny that we are equal by appealing to our differences, for these have nothing to do with that particular idea of equality which those who insist upon it have in mind.

Nor is the claim that all men are equal based on the fact that we all belong to the same species, and share the same biological make-up and the same morphological and physiological traits. If it were, one might equally well say, 'all geese are equal', or 'all flies are equal', or 'all nettles are equal'. But we do not say these things, indeed we are not sure quite what they would mean if we did say them. It is people who are equal, not flies.

Enlightenment thinkers believed that people are all born the same, like empty slates, and that all our differences proceed from our upbringing and the influence of our environment. Today we can no longer believe this, for we know that people are born with different kinds of genetic make-up, and although in the field of human genetics there is still much that remains to be studied and explained, there is no doubt that we differ from one another by our inherited traits, and not only by our upbringing: we are the product of both. One cannot claim that Hitler's entire career was already detailed in his genes, or that Mother Theresa's every thought and deed was engraved on hers; one may, however, fairly safely assume that there are certain inherited traits which make it possible – although not necessary – for someone to become rather more like Mother Theresa than Hitler, or rather more like Hitler than Mother Theresa. But both Hitler and Mother Theresa, in addition to belonging to the same species, are, in a certain sense – in just that very sense which we want to explain – the same: they are *equal*, albeit highly dissimilar.

One can certainly appeal to the Christian – but not only the Christian – religious tradition in order to justify the claim that all men are equal. It is this tradition we have in mind when we say that all men are the children of one father, and will be judged by God according to the same measure, rich and poor alike, whatever their status or education or class or place of birth. In this sense we are all equal as moral subjects to whom God has revealed certain commandments of natural law and whom He has endowed with the free will to keep or break those commandments.

But can one proclaim the equality of all men as a fact, and not only as an injunction, independently of the belief that we are all one in the eyes of God? I think one can, but it requires certain assumptions of a moral nature, assumptions which also concern the constitution of man himself. When we say that all men are equal we mean that they are equal in human dignity, which we all possess and which no one has the right to violate. But what is this human dignity which we all have, and which, according to some philosophers, is inseparable from our ability to think and to make free choices, in particular the choice between good and evil? It is certainly not anything we can see, and it is easier to tell when it has been violated than to describe what it is.

We may be able to see our way more clearly if we limit ourselves to one aspect of the problem, namely to our conception of man as a being which is able, of its own accord and independently of external pressures and circumstances, to choose between good and evil. (We shall not go into the special case of the severely handicapped who are incapable of any kind of participation in society and totally dependent on others.) People are clearly capable of making choices and taking responsibility for what they do, whether they do good or evil; it is the possession of this ability, and not the way in which it is used, that makes them equal in dignity. Humanity as a whole, by this description, is worthy of respect, and so, accordingly, is every human being in his own right. There is nothing particularly controversial in any of this. But does it imply anything specific about the way we should treat those who use their freedom to kill or torture, to violate, humiliate or trample on the dignity of others? Surely just this: that even the worst human beings, those who must be punished or imprisoned for their crimes, must be accorded human dignity, for this dignity is independent of all that distinguishes people from one another – their sex, their race and their nationality, their education, their profession and their character.

If we believed ourselves to be mere automatons whose thoughts and deeds inevitably depend entirely on external forces and circumstances, on the physical world, then indeed the concept of dignity, and therefore also that of equality, would have no sense.

From the fact that we are equal in the way I have described it must follow that inequality in the eyes of the law is indeed counter to human dignity. It does not follow, however, that we have the right to demand equality in the sense of an equal distribution of goods. This kind of equality has of course often been proclaimed, first by certain medieval sects, later by the Jacobin left during the French revolution, and from the nineteenth century onwards by various groups within the socialist movement. Their reasoning was simple: since people are equal, everyone deserves an equal share of all earthly goods. Indeed, in some varieties of egalitarianism it was assumed that since equality is the highest value, it must remain our goal even where everyone, including the poorest, will be worse off through it. Never mind that even the poorest will end up poorer than they were before: the main thing was that no one should be better off than anyone else. But this reasoning is flawed. Such ideologies are not concerned with bettering people's lot, only with making sure that no one's lot is better than anyone else's; they are inspired not by a sense of justice but by envy. There is an anecdote about a Russian peasant to whom God says, 'I will give you anything you want, but whatever you ask for and receive, your neighbour will get twice as much. What would you like?' And the peasant replies: 'Please, God, pluck out one of my eyes.' Here is true egalitarianism.

This ideal of equality, however, is impossible to realize. If it were to be put into practice, the entire economy would have to be subject to totalitarian controls; everything would have to be planned by the state; no one would be allowed to undertake any sort of activity except at the state's command; and in consequence no one would have any reason to exert himself unless forced to do so. As a result the entire economy would collapse, but there would still be no equality: we know by experience that in a totalitarian regime inequality is unavoidable, for those who govern, if they are not subject to any form of social control, will always allocate the lion's share of material goods to themselves. They will also take control of other goods which, although not material, are equally if not more important, such as access to information and participation in government; these will be unavailable to the great majority of the population. Thus the final result will be both poverty and repression.

One might, of course, ask whether equality in the distribution of goods could not be achieved on a voluntary basis, as it is in a monastery or on a kibbutz. The answer is simple: it could, in the sense that such a system would not violate any laws of physics or chemistry. But it would, unfortunately, contradict all that we know about human behaviour, at least of the typical kind.

This does not imply, however, that inequality in the distribution of goods is not a serious and worrying problem, especially where there is dreadful poverty on a great scale. Progressive taxes have so far proved the most effective way of softening such inequality, but beyond a certain point they have disastrous effects on the economy, to the detriment of the poor as well as the rich. We must therefore accept that certain rules of economic life cannot simply be annulled. Of course, it is extremely important that everyone should be able to enjoy the essentials of what we call a decent life: food, clothes to put on one's back, a home, access to medical care and an education for one's children. In civilized countries these principles are generally accepted, albeit imperfectly realized. But any attempt to achieve full equality in the distribution of goods is a recipe for disaster – for everyone. The market may not be just, but abolishing the market leads to poverty and oppression. Equality in human dignity, on the other hand, and the equality of rights and duties that follows from it, is an essential requirement if we are not to degenerate into barbarians. Without it we could, for example, decide that other races or nations may be exterminated with impunity; that there is no reason to grant women the same civil rights as men; that the old and infirm who are of no use to society may simply be killed; and so on. Our belief in this equality not only protects our civilization; it is what makes us human beings.

4
ON LYING

The deliberate transmission of false information is, so to speak, part of the natural order of things. The butterfly says to the bird, 'But I'm not really a butterfly at all, I'm just a dead leaf'; the wasp says to the bee guarding its hive, 'But I'm not really a wasp at all, I'm a bee ... You can see for yourself, dear bee,' it adds in a scholarly way, 'with the help of your olfactory organs' (apparently there are varieties of wasp which actually do this). The difference between these two types of falsehood is immediately apparent: we praise the butterfly, because by pretending to be a dead leaf it is trying to protect itself from a predator which might otherwise have it for supper; but we condemn the wasp, because it is only pretending to be a bee in order to get into the hive and rob the bees of the hard-earned fruit of their labours.

We make similar moral judgements about the lies told by people: some shock us, while others seem justifiable. Some philosophers, most notably Kant and St Augustine, have defended extreme moral positions in which lying is strictly forbidden in any circumstances. But a moral imperative which says that we must never lie, whatever the circumstances, is not only unlikely to be fulfilled; in some circumstances it can conflict with other imperatives, such as kindness to our fellow-men, or with the public interest. War naturally comes to mind as one such circumstance, for deceiving the enemy is an essential part of the art of warfare; so do diplomacy and business. But the simplest example, taken from real life, comes from the period of occupation during the Second World War: if a Jew is hiding in your house, and the SS knocks on your door looking for him, do you, does anyone with a shred of conscience, hand him over to certain death in the name of the noble imperative which enjoins us never to lie?

Governments often lie to their citizens, either directly or by omission. Often they do this in order to avoid criticism and to conceal their mistakes or misdeeds. There are times, however, when a government's lies are justifiable, for they are genuinely in the national interest. Apart from matters of state security, which must be kept secret, such lies might concern the economy: if, for example, a government intends to devalue the currency, it must deny any such intention if asked, otherwise the country would suffer great losses from financial speculators, who would swarm like locusts over the easy gains to be made.

Moreover, there is often a thin line between falsehood and such social virtues as discretion and politeness, but we would all admit that without them life in society would be much worse than it is: far from breathing the pure air of truth, we would stifle in a world of boorishness. We do not appreciate people who make a point of always telling the truth, or what they, rightly or wrongly, consider to be the truth: we call them boors.

A more complicated and much-debated question concerns the veracity of doctors when dealing with the terminally ill: if they do not inform their patients of the hopelessness of their condition, they are lying, whether directly or by omission. The custom varies from country to country, and it is not difficult to find arguments for both sides; but such arguments generally involve appeals to humanitarian principles, to the interests of the patient and his family, not to the value of truth in itself.

In short, common sense tells us that there are circumstances in which lying is indicated in a good cause. The problem is how to define a 'good cause' without extending the definition to cover everything that happens to be in our own interest; not every matter of expediency for us is a 'good cause' for everyone else, and it is hard to conceive of a definition that would cover every imaginable case.

Defenders of a strict moral imperative not to lie say that if everyone told lies simply whenever they felt like it, or whenever it seemed expedient, our trust in other people would be completely undermined; and trust is a necessary condition of our coexistence in an ordered society. They add that the liars would in any case be thwarted by their own lies, since no one would believe anything anyone said.

This is not in itself an unreasonable argument, but as a justification for an absolute moral imperative not to lie it is unconvincing. If we could no longer believe anything anyone said, life would indeed become intolerable; but the total erosion of our mutual trust is an unlikely prospect. We usually know when we can safely rely on what someone tells us and when, on the contrary, a degree of suspicion is indicated, because our interlocutor has reasons of his own for wanting to lead us astray. People rarely lie for no reason. There are, of course, notorious liars: I once knew a writer who liked inventing colourful tales about his life, adapting them each time to each new circumstance and audience; but he did this with such imagination and wit that it would have been churlish to complain. Besides, although his stories were enjoyable to listen to, everyone knew that they should not be taken seriously, so there was no danger that others might suffer because the virtue of truthfulness was so singularly lacking from his character. Then there are pathological liars, who are quite simply unable to tell the truth about anything; they will twist and distort everything without any apparent reason, and also without imagination. But such people tend to be harmless, since no one believes what they say, and we treat them with the contempt they deserve.

Nor does the prevalence of lies in business, politics and war undermine the trust we place in others in our private dealings with them; the people who work in these fields are perfectly well aware of who might want to deceive them and why, and know when to exercise caution. Even the lies told in advertisements are less harmful than they might seem. All countries have laws designed to protect consumers from misrepresentation, and false claims made in advertisements for products are punishable by law. It is illegal, for instance, to market tap water as an infallible cure for cancer. It is not illegal, on the other hand, to claim that Miracle soap or Humbug beer is the best in the world. The difference is that, in the latter case, the advertiser's aim is not to make us believe that Miracle soap or Humbug beer really is the best in the world; it is, rather, to impress on our minds the image of Miracle soap in its distinctive packaging, and nudge us, the next time we have to buy a bar of soap, towards the product that seems familiar after the countless times we have watched it advertised on television. The advertiser is, rightly, counting on our natural tendency toward conservatism; he knows that if he shows us pictures of Miracle soap often enough, we shall feel that it is familiar even if it is not.

When we turn to the kind of lies told in politics, however, there is an important distinction to be made. Lies in politics are a frequent occurrence, but in democratic countries freedom of speech and criticism protects us from some of their harmful effects; the distinction between truth and falsehood remains intact. If a minister disclaims knowledge of something he knew perfectly well, he is lying; but whether or not he is found out, the difference between truth and falsehood remains clear. The same cannot be said of totalitarian countries; in particular it cannot be said of communism in its heyday, the Stalinist era. There the distinction between the true and the politically correct was entirely blurred. As a result, people half came to believe the 'politically correct' slogans which they had been mouthing, from sheer fear, for so long, and even political leaders sometimes fell victim to their own lies. This was precisely the aim: if enough confusion could be caused in people's minds to make them forget the distinction between truth and political correctness, they would come to believe that whatever was politically correct was thereby also necessarily true. In this way an entire nation's historical memory could be altered.

This was not merely an instance of lying: it was an attempt to eradicate altogether the very concept of truth in the normal sense of the word. The attempt was not entirely successful, but the mental devastation it caused was vast, particularly in the Soviet Union. In Poland, where the totalitarian regime had never attained its full potential, the effects were milder, but still deeply felt. Thus freedom of speech and criticism, while it cannot eradicate political lies, can nevertheless restore and protect the normal meanings of the words 'falsehood', 'truth' and 'veracity'.

Although there are circumstances in which lying is permissible or even, in a 'good cause', desirable, it does not follow that we may simply say, 'Sometimes lying is wrong and sometimes it isn't', and leave it at that. This is too vague a principle to be relied upon, for it could be used to justify every instance of lying. Nor does it follow that we should bring up our children according to such a precept. It would be better to teach children that lying is always wrong, whatever the circumstances; in this way they will at least feel uncomfortable when they do lie. The rest they can learn by themselves, quickly, easily and without the help of adults.

But if an absolute injunction against lying is both in-effective and potentially in conflict with other, more important moral imperatives, how are we to go about finding a general principle which will take account of those times when lying is permissible? The answer, as I have said before, is that there is no such principle: no general rule can take account of every conceivable moral circumstance and provide an infallible solution. There are, however, certain morals which we may draw from considering the question, and which may prove helpful.

The first moral is that we should make an effort not to lie to ourselves. This means, among other things, that when we lie we should be aware of the fact. Self-deception is a separate and important subject in itself, and I cannot discuss it here. Suffice it to say that whenever we lie in a good cause, we should know that we are doing so.

Secondly, we should remember that the ways in which we justify our lies to ourselves, and our conception of the 'good cause' in the name of which we lie, are always suspect if the 'good cause' in question happens to coincide with our own interests.

Thirdly, we should keep in mind that even when lying is justified in the name of some other, greater moral good, it is still not itself morally good.

Fourthly and lastly, we should be aware that while lying is often harmful to other people, it is more often harmful to ourselves, for its effects are soul-destroying.

Remembering these four rules will not make us, or even the majority of us, into saints, nor will it eradicate lying from the world. But it may teach us caution when we use lying as a weapon, even when use it we must.

5
ON TOLERATION

The word 'toleration', as we must all have noticed, is a very popular one nowadays. But even as toleration is urged upon us from all sides, the word tends, like so many other popular words, to be used vaguely, carelessly and for a variety of purposes, so that in the end we sometimes lose track of what it really means. While the word itself already existed in classical Latin, the problem of toleration emerged as a social issue in Europe in the sixteenth century, as a result of religious schisms and conflicts. At that time, toleration simply meant not persecuting others for their religious beliefs and practices. The goal of advocates of toleration was therefore to reform the law in such a way that the state could no longer use force to impose the dominant religion. Appeals for toleration in this sense became increasingly numerous, and in a variety of countries edicts were issued to ensure it; but it was not long before these same edicts were annulled, persecutions returned, and calls were once more heard for the punishment of heretics and dissenters from the faith. We know that the history of the religious wars was marked by countless horrors. In the end, however, it is safe to say that in nominally Christian countries the battle for toleration has on the whole been won. This is far from being the case in Islamic countries, where aggressive and intolerant movements are extremely powerful. A tolerant regime is simply a regime which does not impose anything upon its citizens in their choice of religious beliefs and practices. Indeed, the principle whereby the state should abstain from intervening in matters of religion has come to be so widely accepted that even in the communist countries of Europe, including those where churches, the clergy and the faithful were subjected to repression of the harshest kind, it was at least verbally admitted.

All this seems simple and even uncontroversial today, but on closer inspection complications begin to emerge. In order for the principle of toleration in this sense to be accepted and applied, we need not only laws but also the right cultural conditions, and these cannot be manufactured by fiat. Christian advocates of toleration in the sixteenth and seventeenth centuries argued that we should refrain from mutual slaughter in the name of our differences of opinion on the matter of the Holy Trinity, the sacrament of the Eucharist or predestination, since God, at the Last Judgement, will not ask us about our theological opinions, whether right or wrong, but about whether we tried to live by the commandments of the Gospels. Thus it was assumed, and sometimes asserted explicitly, that all dogmatic differences between churches, faiths or sects were unimportant and of no account; from which one might in turn easily have been led to conclude that there was no justification for the existence of any of these churches or sects as distinct and separate bodies. It was less easy, however, to convince the churches themselves of this. (Even though all this took place within the Christian culture, and in relatively tolerant countries, such as seventeenth-century Holland, still open atheism was not tolerated.) Thus it was that a new sense crept into the concept of toleration, namely that of indifference. There is a distinction, however, both cultural and psychological, between saying that it is better to tolerate even great mistakes than to provoke religious wars, and saying that we must tolerate all manner of theological opinions because they are matters of indifference. It is one thing for me to say, 'Your opinions are terrible, wrong and harmful, but for all that I will not cut off your head; I shall leave the matter in the hands of God', and quite another if I say, 'Say what you like about religion, none of it matters anyway.'

When we talk about toleration, however, we are talking not only about laws concerning religion but also about human behaviour and morals. (Today we tend to speak of 'tolerance' rather than 'toleration', but there seems to be little difference between the two.) Thus I can be said to be tolerant if I neither persecute other people nor demand their persecution, and if I refrain from reacting aggressively to things I strongly dislike or disapprove of, or am shocked or repelled by. We use the word in a similar sense in medicine, when we talk about our tolerance to various drugs: since drugs are harmful, when we say that we have such-and-such a tolerance to a particular drug, we mean that our body can accept it to such-and-such a dosage without harmful effects. In France brothels used to be called 'houses of tolerance', the name suggesting that while brothels were not on the whole a good thing, it was better, for various reasons, to tolerate them. In modern France one sometimes sees street signs which say, oddly, 'parking tolerated'; they appear to imply a grudging sort of acceptance, and this is in fact precisely what they are meant to imply, for they are there to indicate that while parking in that sort of spot (usually on the pavement) is not in general allowed, the authorities will put up with it in this particular case – the suggestion being, again, that it is not in general a good sort of thing.

It is important to notice, however, that when tolerance is enjoined upon us nowadays, it is often in the sense of indifference: we are asked, in effect, to refrain from expressing – or indeed holding – any opinion, and sometimes even to condone every conceivable type of behaviour or opinion in others. This kind of tolerance is something entirely different, and demanding it is part of our hedonistic culture, in which nothing really matters to us; it is a philosophy of life without responsibility and without beliefs. It is encouraged by a variety of philosophies in fashion today, which teach us that there is no such thing as truth in the traditional sense, and therefore that when we persist in our beliefs, even if we do so without aggression, we are *ipso facto* sinning against tolerance.

This is nonsense, and harmful nonsense. Contempt for truth harms our civilization no less than fanatical insistence on the truth. In addition, an indifferent majority clears the way for fanatics, of whom there will always be plenty around. Our civilization encourages the belief that everything should be just fun and games – as indeed it is in the infantile philosophies of the so-called 'New Age'. Their content is impossible to describe, for they mean anything one wants them to; that is what they are for.

We have the right to stand by our beliefs. To take an example: in civilized countries the practice of homosexuality is not illegal, as long, of course, as it takes place between consenting adults. The Church considers homosexual practices to be morally wrong and forbidden, on the basis of the Old and the New Testaments, its own tradition and its own theological interpretation of sexuality. Now if the Church were to demand the return of laws banning homosexual practices, it could be accused of gross intolerance. But homosexual organizations demand that the Church withdraw its teachings on homosexuality, and here it is they who are displaying gross intolerance the other way. In England there have been cases of demonstrations and attacks against churches because of this. Who, then, is being intolerant here? Homosexuals who maintain that the Church is in error are free to leave it; nothing stands in their way. But when they want to impose their own opinions on the Church in a brash and aggressive way, they are not protecting tolerance, but advocating intolerance. Tolerance is only effective if it is mutual.

It is sometimes said that people should be punished for their actions, not for their opinions. The trouble is that the line between the two is not always clear. In some countries, for instance, it is illegal to incite racial hatred. But incitement can take many forms, and racists often say in their defence that they were merely expressing an opinion, and one cannot be punished for one's opinions. But verbal expression is also a form of action, and like all actions it can have the worst or the best of effects. If we say no more than this, we may be taken as implying that all opinions should be controlled for their possible effects. If, on the other hand, we do not say it, we are implying that nothing should be illegal if it does not involve violence. We must therefore look for compromise solutions – always uncomfortable, but unavoidable. The same ancient dilemma has plagued the problem of toleration: may we, and should we, tolerate political or religious movements which are hostile to tolerance and seek to destroy all the mechanisms which protect it, totalitarian movements or movements which aim to impose their own despotic regime? Such movements may not be dangerous so long as they are small; then they can be tolerated. But when they expand and increase in strength, they must be tolerated, for by then they are invincible, and in the end an entire society can fall victim to the worst kind of tyranny. Thus it is that unlimited tolerance turns against itself and destroys the very conditions of its own existence. I admit I myself think that movements which aim to destroy freedom should not be tolerated or granted the protection of the law; tolerance is in less danger from the kind of intolerance than lifting such protection involves.

There is no good principle, however, that cannot be turned to bad use. It may be acceptable to ban the expression of racist ideologies, but in America those who research the statistical distribution of various abilities in racially defined populations have been branded and attacked as racists, and this is not acceptable. Such research naturally requires particular care, and is certainly liable to exploitation for purposes of racist propaganda; but banning it on this pretext is far worse than any undesirable effects it may have, for it implies acceptance of the principle that all scientific research should be banned if its results may prove contrary to the accepted ideas of a given age, and this is a totalitarian principle. One should, of course, criticize the results of such research if one has good counter-arguments; but to ban it would be to establish an ideological dictatorship over scientific research.

I repeat: toleration is best protected not so much by the law as by the preservation and strengthening of a tolerant society. We each of us have the potential for intolerance. The need to impose one's own view of the world on others is strong. We would like everyone to believe what we believe, for only then do we feel spiritually on firm ground, and need no longer think about our beliefs or confront them with others. It is because of this that confrontations between different religious, philosophical or political beliefs involve so much aggression. But if intolerance, in other words the desire to convert others to one's beliefs by aggressive or coercive means, were to be eradicated by a way of life in which no one believes anything and nothing matters to anyone except that life should be fun, then we are doomed, for sooner or later we shall fall victim to some sort of ideocracy. Let us not counter praise of coercion with praise of general indifference.

6

ON TRAVEL

Why do we travel, and what do we like about it? It seems a silly question to ask: after all, we all know why we travel. But there are a lot of things which may appear obvious at first glance and later turn out not to be so obvious after all. Is travelling an instinctive type of behaviour, and if so, what kind of instinct inspires it? Do we enjoy travelling because it allows us to experience something new, and is it simply this newness that attracts us? And if so, is that not an odd kind of enjoyment?

The experience of many generations, no doubt instilled in us through some process of evolution, has taught us that the world is not a friendly place. We have learned that it is prudent, in such a world, to distrust the new and unknown, and value rather the safe and the familiar, staying quietly in our own little corner without straying from beaten paths. But we do not do this. Why are children so fond of books about travels? And why is it that, when the ink was barely dry on our maps after all the blank spaces had been filled in, people rushed off once more to launch themselves into travels in space, travels of a kind hardly imaginable even a short time ago, and continue to dream of exploring even more distant spaces?

When we talk about travel we mean, of course, not just any kind of moving about from one place to another, but the kind of moving about where the journey itself is the goal; we are not talking about the kind of travelling we have to do in order to accomplish something that we would, if we could, far rather have accomplished at home, without all the bother and inconvenience that travel entails. The businessmen who arrange conferences at airports and return to their offices immediately afterwards are not travelling at all, merely transacting business which they prefer, and indeed nowadays often do manage, to transact at home. Nor am I sure whether travel is the word to describe the kind of mass tourism where, for example, inhabitants of cold countries such as England migrate to Spain in search of some warmth and a bit of sea, safe in the knowledge that English bars and English food (God preserve us) already await them there, in Spain itself and have no interest at all. The kind of traveller we are talking about sets out on his travels wanting to experience some-thing new and unfamiliar, just because it IS new and unfamiliar.

When we travel we are not, strictly speaking, setting

out to learn something; most of the things we learn
through our travels can easily – often more easily – be
learnt at home. As Horace said, *'Caelum non animum
mutant qui trans mare currunt'* – ('They change their
sky, and not themselves, who scour across the sea') – in
other words, we will not attain wisdom by running about
from one place to another. We do not, then, travel for
knowledge. Nor do we travel in order to forget, for a short
while, our daily cares and troubles, for we know (Horace
again) that *'post equitem sedet atra cura'* – ('behind the
horseman sits black care') – in other words, wherever we
go, our cares will go with us. Thus it is not a thirst for
knowledge that drives us, nor a longing to escape, but
simple curiosity; and curiosity seems to be a driving force
of its own, not explicable in terms of any others. Those
who have studied such things tell us that curiosity, the
disinterested need to find out about things, is an instinct
that remains with us all our lives, and a uniquely human
characteristic.

We are curious about the unfamiliar not because we
expect to derive any benefit from it, or because we feel
threatened by it and want to prevent it from harming us
in some way; we are simply curious. People do many
things they know to be dangerous from sheer curiosity:
they travel to unfamiliar and hostile regions, where they
are sometimes killed scaling mountains or exploring
caves. It was because of our curiosity that we were

expelled from the Garden of Eden, and theologians used to condemn curiosity itself as sinful. But without this sinful impulse there would be few changes in our lives, and little progress.

Nowadays one sometimes comes across the opinion that there was no such thing as the 'discovery of America', because by the time European travellers reached American shores the Red Indians had already been living there for a long time, and did not need to have their own country discovered. But this is a silly objection, because if people live isolated from one another, and ignorant of one another's ways, one may indeed say that they have 'discovered' one another when they finally meet; and if the Americans had made quicker progress at navigation and reached Europe first, it would have been true to say that they discovered Europe. Even today, when, impelled by curiosity, we travel to some country or city unknown to us, we talk of discovering it for ourselves; to discover something in this sense is simply to experience something new, and need not involve the acquisition of knowledge that no one has ever possessed before. The sentimental journeys we sometimes make to the places of our childhood, places we know well but have long since left behind, are surely also a kind of travel, and a kind of discovery; for even if, on the face of it, we do not seem to be experiencing anything new on such journeys, we are in a sense returning to ourselves as we were long ago in the past: it is as if we were travelling in time, and to travel in time in this way is to experience as new something that was once familiar.

Thus we feel the need of new experiences simply because they are new, and not because of anything else about them: it is their newness itself that draws us. And if we are drawn by newness, it is because of our particular, uniquely human way of experiencing time. We would always like to be in at the start of things: to feel that the world lies open to us, that it has only just begun. The experience of newness gives us such a feeling, however illusory. Perhaps this is why people change husbands and wives: it allows them to experience, for a moment, a new time, another beginning.

It would surely be wrong to suppose that curiosity, or the need for newness, accompanies us all to the same extent, always and everywhere. If it did, our lives would be impossible. In all forms of life, instincts of conservation, which aim to preserve the existing order, coexist with instincts that aim at evolution. In us humans these two opposing forces are expressed in our need for safety, stability and familiarity on the one hand, and our need for newness and change, in other words our curiosity, on the other. These tendencies are contradictory, but both are an essential part of what makes us human. One of the things that distinguish human personalities is the degree to which these conflicting tendencies are present in them: we distinguish between people who cling to routine and familiarity from those who feel stifled by routine and long only for change.

Finally, it is worth noting that our curiosity, our need to seek out the new and unfamiliar, presupposes, whether or not we are aware of it, a certain view of the world – a certain 'philosophy'. Namely, it presupposes that the world of our experience, this world that we are so curious about, has some value. If, like true Buddhists, we really believed that the world is worthless and filled only with pain and suffering; that in every significant respect it is always the same, and no differences are of any account; that there is nothing new under the sun, and that the history of mankind is nothing but a monotonous repetition of the same pain and suffering – if we really believed all this, then we would feel no curiosity, no need to experience the new, and therefore no desire to travel.

But the question of whether the Buddhists are right is not one that we will explore. For to do so would be to descend into the murky depths of metaphysics, and that is not something it behoves us to do when engaged in reflections on a subject as frivolous as travel.

7

ON VIRTUE

What do we mean when we talk about virtue? We talk about different sorts of virtues related to particular activities: civic virtues, intellectual virtues, and so on. We might say that virtues in this sense are skills which have a moral content: they are morally valuable. We also talk about virtue in general, meaning that collection of morally valuable skills which not only make us better people but also improve our relations with others: they make us good and they make our lives good.

Nowadays one rarely hears references to 'maidenly virtues', 'losing one's virtue', 'women of easy virtue', and so on – phrases associated in our minds with Victorian ideals of chastity which our age finds faintly ridiculous. Perhaps because of this association with past ideals, the word 'virtue' has acquired a slightly tarnished air. This is a pity, for the word 'virtue' has many virtues, and it is high time that we recognized them. We have, after all, no other word to describe an aggregate of moral skills.

We do not need a word with as broad a definition as the Greek *arete*, which could be applied to any positive quality of objects as well as people: the virtue of a knife, for instance, is that it cuts well, and the virtue of a field that it yields a good harvest. Nor do we need one with as narrow a definition as the Latin *virtus*, which referred mainly to virility. But the English 'virtue' is a word we can put to good use.

How many different virtues there are, and how to classify them, is not a question that need concern us here. What is worth noticing, however, is that virtues, if defined in the way I have suggested, as moral skills essential for life in a human community, in one important respect resemble other, non-moral skills.

We learn virtues by being brought up in a community where they are practised, in the same way as we learn to swim, or to use a knife and fork. We cannot learn to swim without going into the water; nor can a child learn to use a knife and fork by reading a series of complicated instructions about the precise angle at which his fingers should hold them. In the same way, a handbook of virtues would be useless in a community where those virtues were not practised. When virtues die out, human society dies with them, and no amount of handbooks will help. A priest may quote the Gospels from the pulpit, but if he spouts threats and curses and is seen to be full of hate, he will not inculcate Christian virtues in his flock;

on the contrary, by his own behaviour he will undermine
and destroy the very virtues he preaches. Similarly the
rich financier who fulminates against human greed –
unless he uses his wealth to benefit others.

Virtues, then, are learnt not from textbooks but from
living among people who practise them. But can all the
virtues ever be present in any one person? The Stoics
thought that they could. They believed that virtue is its
own reward: the just man's reward, for example, is the
fact that he is just. For the Stoics, a virtue was a true
virtue only if it was practised for its own sake; if a man
practises justice in the hope of some other reward, he is
not truly just. It follows from this that if we lack one
virtue, we lack them all; conversely, if we have one, we
have all the others too. Having some virtues but not
others would imply that we practise virtues not for their
own sake but for some other reason related to our own
benefit or convenience, and then they would not be true
virtues. Conversely, practising virtues only for their own
sake, just because they are good, implies that we practise
them all, for we would have no reason to practise only
some and not others.

Such an all-or-nothing view of virtue is a very restrictive one; it is also extremely hard to maintain. To say that
we must have all the virtues if we are to have any at all
is to imply that we can be either absolutely perfect or
utterly worthless and corrupt, but nothing in between. It

is unwise educational strategy to present people with a choice between being perfection incarnate and being rotten to the core, for they are then liable to say to themselves, well, if I can't be perfection incarnate, it doesn't matter what I do; and I certainly can't be perfection incarnate, so I might as well do whatever I please.

The Stoic view of virtue, then, is restrictive and dangerous. It is also false, for there is nothing contradictory in supposing that people can possess certain virtues – virtues in the true sense, practised not from calculation but for their own sake – while lacking others. One can be just and prudent but not brave; truthful and kind to others but not industrious; and so on. The only grain of truth we can salvage from the Stoic theory is that virtues do seem to strengthen one another: if we already possess some, we do seem to be better at acquiring others. If we set about trying to be just, for instance, we soon find that we must also be persevering and brave. So virtues are not, after all, as independent of one another as they may seem.

A rigid all-or-nothing attitude to virtue is not only -educationally counter-productive; it is also liable to slide into fanaticism. Absolutism in the practice of virtues can be harmful: if one practises and encourages virtues always and everywhere, regardless of the circumstances, one can make life intolerable both for oneself and for others. Courage, with such an attitude, can degenerate into mere recklessness; justice, rigorously applied and blind to mitigating circumstances of any kind, can be mere cruelty, inflicted not by the truly just but by the self-satisfied and proud; truthfulness becomes brutality and insensitivity to the suffering and misfortunes of others; the laudable principle of sparing others pain and distress can lead to blanket indulgence of evil. Even wisdom can be no more than a pretext for escaping the inevitable conflicts and vicissitudes of life. People brought up in warlike tribes learn courage and physical endurance, but often cruelty as well; people who toil at academic pursuits and possess all the intellectual virtues sometimes close their eyes to what is going on around them, partly from a conviction that their work is more important and partly from a reluctance to involve themselves in the conflicts that inevitably arise when one becomes engaged in social issues. But the civic virtues that they lack can also be taken to excess: the sense of social responsibility that drives some people to involve themselves in public life can degenerate into an aggressive insistence on the rightness of one's own point of view to the exclusion of all others, and an inability to distinguish between the trivial and the genuinely important.

It is also worth noticing that although all virtues are liable to degenerate into counter-virtues, some are more prone to this than others. Thus respect for the truth, for instance, seems more likely to degenerate into fanaticism than, say, kindness to others, especially if one is convinced of the truth of one's own opinions; and courage holds greater dangers than a capacity for forgiveness.

Of course not all our virtues are merely a cover for our own egoism, as La Rochefoucauld claimed; but it is true that good can always be turned to evil, without our noticing that anything is amiss. This is not a particularly new or striking observation, but it bears repeating as a reminder that we should always be on guard against self-deception and self-satisfaction, and scrupulous in examining the true motives of our actions. We cannot expect everyone to be perfect, or to be identical, which comes to the same thing; but we should be aware that practising virtues requires flexibility and an understanding of the infinite complexity of human affairs. Such an understanding can only come from experience. This is not as hard as it sounds: when virtue is analysed in a textbook way, it starts to seem more complicated than it really is. In real life acquiring virtues is a simple matter, for true virtue is a natural skill, learnt through our own experience of life and its conflicting demands, and through the society of good and thoughtful people.

8

ON COLLECTIVE
RESPONSIBILITY

The phrase 'collective responsibility' is bound up, in our minds, with associations of the worst kind. It conjures up visions of occupying powers murdering people at random in revenge for attempts at resistance; of hostages taken and killed; of terrorist attacks in which hundreds of people, quite uninvolved in whatever it was all about, end up dead; of hatred for whole nations, peoples or races because of the wrongs, real or imaginary, that we feel we have suffered at the hands of some of their members. But we shall not consider cases of this kind here, for they are too obvious.

It has sometimes been said that Christian teaching about original sin also involves the idea of collective responsibility, since according to it we must all suffer for the sins of two people from some distant and ill-defined past whom we have never even met. But there is a distinction to be made here. If we assume, like some Christian theologians, that Adam and Eve passed down to us not only a permanent flaw in our nature but also the real moral burden of their guilt, thus making us true participants in a sin which we nevertheless did not commit, and that all the ills that befall us in this world are God's punishment for that sin, then yes, we are indeed assuming true collective responsibility. Christian humanists found this assumption unacceptable because it seemed to portray God as a merciless tyrant rather than a loving father, and our own sense of ordinary justice naturally rebels against it. If, however, Christian teaching on original sin does not involve such an assumption, but states merely that human nature was permanently warped by the original sin, and we have simply inherited it in its warped state, then the situation is no different than if we had been born with an hereditary disease: it may be dreadful for us, but we don't see it in terms of guilt and punishment. And indeed, the Church of Rome today does not teach that we have inherited the guilt itself, only the flaw in our nature which often tempts us to sin. But it does not force us to sin; we can resist the temptation. Thus we are responsible for our own sins, but not for those of our ancestors. Evil is man's creation, and the suffering that people inflict on one another is man's creation; as for the suffering caused by nature itself, without man's help, one can suppose that nature, too, was warped by the original sin, and the sufferings it inflicts upon us are not a punishment in the proper sense.

Is there, then, any sense in which the idea of collective responsibility can be defended? Can we, without going against our sense of ordinary justice, hold someone responsible for something he did not himself do? I think there is, and we can.

Each one of us belongs to a variety of human collectivities which retain their identity even as their membership changes: a nation, a Church, a social or political organization, or an institution, such as a school, a hospital, a university or a city. We naturally identify with these bodies, for we feel that our fate is bound up with theirs. We feel this not only because we are personally affected, enriched or diminished, by their failures or successes, but also because we see them as moral entities of a certain kind, and therefore as something precious. The ties that bind us to them and to others within them are not based only on a calculation of gains and losses, but on a belief in a common destiny and a disinterested solidarity, which we acknowledge even when we sin against it. So it is surely natural for us to feel concerned in the doings, good or bad, present or past, of the collective body to which we belong; and to feel that they concern us not only because our own, material interests are involved, but also because we care about that collective body as a whole. We have, in other words, a moral interest in it. Admittedly, we find it easier to participate in its worthier achievements and its successes than to share in its ignominy or its defeat. Sports fans may rejoice in the victories of their local or national clubs as if they themselves had done the playing, but they do not have the same sense of participation in defeat, however keenly they may feel it: it was not they, after all, who lost the match. We tend to lose our sense of symmetry in the way we see these things: if the result, or the cause, is a good one, we like to feel we have a share in it; if it is bad, we prefer to blame others.

But victory or defeat on the playing field has little to do with moral responsibility, and that is a more difficult problem. Perhaps the most important issue under that heading is that of national responsibility. Every European nation (except, of course, one's own) has some shameful episodes in its past which it would prefer to forget. Can we DEMAND that people who were not themselves in any way involved in these episodes should feel guilty or ashamed? Do we have the right to insist that Germans born after the war or shortly before it, now in their sixties, should feel responsible for Hitler's crimes? That Americans should feel guilty about slavery or the extermination of the Red Indians, the English about child labour in the Victorian era, the Poles about religious persecution in the seventeenth century or about their country's dreadful treatment of national minorities in the inter-war period? The answer, I think, is that we cannot demand this of others, but we can, and should, demand it of ourselves, for our spiritual well-being. In reality, of course, we tend to do the opposite, demanding it of others but exonerating ourselves on the pretext that we do not believe in collective responsibility.

We are not personally responsible for what our ancestors did, but if we believe that a nation is a moral and spiritual entity which retains its identity over time, even as generations die and others take their place, then we are surely also right to believe that collective responsibility, the responsibility of nations as continuous entities, exists alongside the responsibility of individuals. One might compare this to inheriting the debts as well as the assets of one's parents, except that we are free to accept or refuse an inheritance, and while a refusal on our part is not necessarily viewed in a bad light, if we accept it we are legally bound to pay off the debts. The analogy is flawed on two counts: we are not legally responsible for the sins of our ancestors, and we cannot refuse our inheritance if we accept our membership in the collectivity that we call a nation. Thus we are not legally bound to accept responsibility, and others have no right to demand it of us; but if we do not assume the burden of this responsibility, and the burden of guilt and shame that may accompany it, then the spiritual health of the nation will suffer. The shadow of our falsity will follow us everywhere, and when the time comes for us once again to defend our national dignity, we shall be unable to offer any resistance.

The case of religious bodies seems analogous. It is in the interests of the spiritual well-being of a Church if it can say (as the Church of Rome, to its credit, has said) that it regrets the wrongs, persecutions and crimes perpetrated in its name in the past, and is ashamed of them, instead of contenting itself with saying, 'it wasn't us, it was someone else.' The Church is a continuous collective organism which has existed for centuries; internally it is far better organized than a nation. Past misdeeds committed in its name are therefore its misdeeds, not those of anonymous forces or individuals long dead.

But could we not avoid all this by saying to ourselves that we belong to no nation or church or morally continuous collective entity of any kind; that we care nothing for the successes and failures, the rights and wrongs, of the past; that we are concerned only with our own interests? We could indeed say this, but we could not in good faith believe it. If we openly refused to participate in collective bodies of any kind and felt no solidarity towards anything, we could still live, but it would be a zoor sort of life, in which we could not expect help or solidarity from others when misfortunes befell us, as they befall us all at one time or another; we would be wretched and miserable, for our indifference towards others would be repaid in kind, and we would not be able to complain.

We are born in circumstances quite independent of us. This is natural. Later, when we are able to act for ourselves, the circumstances in which we do so are still to a great degree, although not entirely, independent of us; and yet we must take responsibility for them. This, too, is natural.

9
ON THE WHEEL
OF FORTUNE

There are people who say that playing the lottery or roulette is a silly thing to do, because the odds will always be against us; and then there are those who say that it is immoral. Their criticism is worth thinking about, for it raises questions which touch on an important issue in our lives.

Of course we all know that in any lottery or game of chance the odds are against us, otherwise such games could not exist. Indeed, organizers of lotteries quite often announce the probability of winning the jackpot, and it is always tiny. But if in spite of this we still decide to play, does it follow that we are acting irrationally or unwisely? Not at all. The odds against us may be enormous, but so, proportionally, is the possible gain; why, then, should it be irrational to want to 'try one's luck'? It only becomes irrational if we become addicted to the game as to a drug, and end up ruining ourselves in order to sustain our habit. But most people manage to avoid this, and spend only a small part of their income on such sinful pleasures. The odds may be against us, but do we not, in the course of ordinary life, often find ourselves battling against great odds without, for all that, becoming discouraged? The only difference between games of chance and the odds we sometimes face in ordinary life is that the odds in games of chance can be calculated with great precision, and there is nothing we can do to tilt the balance in our favour.

But is this really so? Some people believe that, through some mysterious relationship or affinity with numbers, they can give fortune a nudge in their favour: they see some numbers as friendly and others as hostile, and claim to be able to manipulate the lottery or games of roulette in their favour by always putting their stake on the friendly ones. Such beliefs are generally viewed as superstitions of a particularly absurd variety, but they seem also to belong to that class of superstitions which it is almost impossible to eradicate.

Others still believe that some people are able to move or direct objects by some sort of psychokinesis, and thus also to influence the roulette wheel or the lottery bag to produce the required numbers; but if there really are such people, they will certainly make sure that their talents in this regard remain well hidden.

There does, in fact, seem to be something in our cerebral make-up that rebels against the very idea of chance.

There are two things we don't like about chance. Physicists used to tell us that all events were precisely defined by the conditions in which they take place, and that probability was only a measure of our own ignorance, for we can never fully grasp those conditions. Now they tell us that probability is itself a feature of the world, and is built into reality. This is something we find hard to understand, and we don't like it. But even more disturbing, perhaps, is the theory that the world consists of nothing but random events, that there is no sense in it, no ultimate goal towards which it is progressing. We don't like this either, and find it depressing. We know, of course, that all progress, all the effort and achievement of civilization, is based on reducing as much as possible the element of chance in the events that concern us, and that we can, to some – often to a considerable – degree, succeed in forcing nature to obey us. But our success is the result of our own – human – intention, our own will. And yet unceasingly, and from time immemorial, the evolution of our world has been accompanied by the belief that the chance events which constitute a part of the ordinary course of our lives are not quirks of fate at all, but rather expressions of a divine will or design, and that this design, while not plainly visible, may nevertheless, with a bit of effort, be discerned. Thus it is not by a quirk of fate but by the will of a higher power that Cecil won the lottery while Basil choked on a bone and died: you just have to know how to decipher the design.

But here we encounter a difficulty. People have managed to invent codes that are unbreakable by analytic means, codes that cannot be deciphered without a key. Such codes are easy to use: they merely require that the sender and the recipient both have in their possession the same extremely long string of random numbers or random arrangements of ones and zeros; all the aspiring code-breaker then has to go on is this enormously long string of random ones and zeros, and no analysis of them will get him anywhere, no matter how long the encoded text: to read it he needs the key. But if people can create unbreakable codes, then (one can argue) so, surely, can God, if He has decided to conceal His designs. And if He has so decided, then all our efforts to decipher His intentions by examining sequences of random events are futile; the key to the code is safely hidden away, and we cannot know why Cecil and not Basil won the lottery. And yet, in spite of this, people continue relentlessly to search for hidden meanings in random events: they always have and they always will.

But here, as in many other matters, our hearts conflict with our heads, and our instincts pull us in different directions. As rational beings we are repelled by randomness, and want to make sense out of the chaos of the world by discovering the true meaning of events rather than merely imposing our own interpretation upon them. In our hearts, however, we feel the lure of the unknown, the gamble, the risk. We like to challenge fate and launch ourselves into risky projects whose outcome is uncertain; and if we did not feel this pull, most of the great achievements of the human race would probably not have come about. This pull was felt not only by the great explorers and discoverers of new lands, by initiators of wars and by great social reformers, but also by writers and poets, by scholars and by scientists – by all those who sought to venture down new and undiscovered paths. But each one of us, at some point in our lives, also feels it: we feel it when we decide to have children, or to study medicine, or when we sit for the first time behind the wheel of a car. Each of those decisions involves risk. We have two souls: one which wants only peace and quiet and safety, and another which seeks the thrill of the dangerous and the unknown.

Thus playing the lottery is not a sign of irrationality. But is it immoral? Those who think so consider that in playing the lottery we are seeking to obtain goods which are not ours to have and which we have not earned; they feel there is something wrong in acquiring great wealth undeservedly, with no work or effort on our part. This is why some clergymen condemn the lottery industry; they assume, although they do not always say so in so many words, that God wants us to acquire the good things in life through our own efforts and ingenuity. Communist countries had no lottery until the slow disintegration of communism was well under way, and the ostensible ideological justification for its absence was similar: people should earn better lives through their own efforts rather than trust to blind fate to help them. But the true ideological justification was different: for although a lottery industry would bring in considerable revenue for the state, it would also provide extra revenue for some individuals, independently of what the state provided; and this was unacceptable. It was unacceptable not because of what were, by then, no more than dusty remnants of the old egalitarian ideologies – although they, too, were probably involved – but because it was, or is, a principle of communism that the state should be the provider and distributor of all goods, and that whatever we have, we have only thanks to its generosity.

But is it, in fact, immoral to enjoy goods which one has not earned oneself? There is room for doubt. When we inherit material goods from our ancestors, we have also not earned them; but a world without inheritance, such as the anarchists once wanted, would be inconceivable; the number of changes that would have to be made to bring it about would be unimaginably vast. Similarly, we have not earned any of the innate talents or abilities with which the genetic lottery has endowed us, even though we generally have to work quite hard in order to make full use of them. Great mathematical or musical talent, for example, although it involves application and effort if it is to bear fruit, also contains a considerable genetic element. We all know that a beautiful woman generally has an easier life than one whom fate has stintingly endowed in this respect, even though she too must make an effort to preserve her beauty, just as a chess master must work hard at his game even though some part of his talent is innate. Making use of goods we have not earned cannot by itself be considered immoral, since there is no principle of justice that governs their random distribution, unless it be God's design, which in any case we can never fathom. Winning the jackpot in the lottery admittedly requires no effort at all, and for this reason may seem more unfair than an inherited talent; but saying that it is 'more unfair' does not get us anywhere, because 'fairness' is not a category that is applicable to randomness. In other words, random events can be favourable or unfavourable, but they cannot be fair or unfair.

10
ON BETRAYAL

We are all born members of an ethnic community. Our membership of that community is a fact independent of us: we do not choose our nation, any more than we choose our family. Our later relationships with people, on the other hand – social, political, professional or sexual – are for the most part the result of our own choice.

It might seem that the position into which we are born, because it was presented to us as a fact, independently of our will, is not binding; in other words, that it entails no responsibilities. After all, we did not sign up for membership of our nation, and we did not ask our parents to bring us into the world. We might think, therefore, that we are bound only by those relationships which we ourselves have chosen. In reality, however, we tend to feel the opposite: we feel bound by unconditional loyalty towards our country and our family, and see their betrayal as the worst of sins; but we feel free to abandon, without fear of disapproval, those human relationships which we ourselves have freely chosen – our membership of a political organization, for example.

A third form of loyalty, which falls somewhere between these two, is our loyalty to our church or religious community. It occupies the middle ground because, although our religious affiliation is not something that is in our blood (as St Jerome said, people are not born Christians, they become Christians), in the overwhelming majority of cases it is decided for us by the environment into which we are born; and wherever it is customary to christen babies shortly after their birth, as it is in the Roman Church, for example, people almost always adopt the religion of their parents. Conversion or apostasy is accordingly condemned by one's original religious community. In Islam it is a crime that invariably incurs the death penalty.

It should not surprise us, however, that betrayal of a community to which one belongs not by choice but by accident of birth should entail such harsh condemnation. A nation, like an individual, is the creation of nature, not a thing of human design, and as such does not need to justify its existence. It exists simply because it exists; it is its own justification. Likewise the individual: his existence contains its own legitimacy. Our belonging to a nation, inasmuch as it is not the result of our own choice, is something that we always carry within us; if we reject it or deny its legitimacy, it is as if we were annihilating that nation itself.

This is not true of bodies to which we belong through our own choice, such as churches (although, as I have mentioned above, they fall into a category of their own) or political parties. Bodies such as these do need to justify their existence, because they are there for a specific purpose, and their validity lies in the fulfilment of that purpose. The Church exists in order to spread the truth and distribute the goods necessary for eternal salvation. Political parties also exist in order to spread their truth and harness energy for a declared purpose – namely, to attain temporary salvation by building an ideal world and destroying its enemies, or at least to better the lot of mankind through concrete measures of one kind or another. Let us suppose that I belong to a certain sect. At some point I discover that I have been deceived: the head of the sect turns out to be a charlatan, a con-man out to cheat people of their money and receive sexual favours from them by persuading them that he is God. So I leave the sect – in other words, I betray it. In the same way I can leave, and thus betray, a political party, if I discover that its real aim is slavery rather than freedom. In such cases the word 'betrayal' tends to be used only by members of the sect or party in question, for it is not a neutral word, but laden with condemnation; most of us would not condemn someone for leaving some sect founded by an unscrupulous madman, or for leaving the fascist or the communist party. Our use of the word 'betrayal' excludes the possibility that betrayal can be a good thing because the body that has been betrayed deserves nothing better; it entails disapproval.

It follows that only our own opinion of the thing or person betrayed can guide us in determining whether a particular action is or is not an act of betrayal. A German who worked for the Allies during the war, for example, was collaborating with the enemies of his country, the Nazi state; but we do not call him a traitor. On the contrary, we think that he showed courage in defending a just cause. In other words, we decide whether or not a particular action is an act of betrayal according to what we consider to be our moral duty, or at least morally right.

It quickly becomes apparent, however, that such a definition embroils us in a tangle of ambiguities. For we are reluctant to concede that some acts of betrayal can be morally right only because we have already loaded the concept of betrayal with our own moral and political opinions, and these are not necessarily obvious. Deliberately causing the death of someone who had a right to expect our loyalty is a particularly glaring and repellent instance of betrayal, and that is why both Judas and Brutus occupy the lowest circle of Dante's inferno. But surely Hitler, too, had a right to expect loyalty from his generals; and yet we would not consign to the same place those generals who tried to kill him.

One way out of the difficulty is to say that a nation and a state are different things, and that we may, in the name of the nation, reject or betray a state which is an instrument of evil, even if that state is a sovereign one and has the support of the majority of the nation, as in the case of Hitler's Germany or Stalin's Soviet Union, but not of Eastern and Central Europe after the Second World War. In this day and age it would be difficult simply to go on repeating: 'my country right or wrong'. In the nineteenth century it was easier: one felt that it was wrong to betray king and country whatever their rights and wrongs, as long, of course, as the country really was one's own, and not occupied by a foreign power. In the twentieth century, however, the criterion is no longer tradition or national loyalty but ideology: if the ideology is correct, treason is not treason.

We cannot even say without qualification that betrayal is permissible if the state in question is not a legitimate one, for the criteria of a state's legitimacy are by no means clear. In international law a state is legitimate if it is recognized by the so-called international community, in other words the United Nations. But among the states recognized by the United Nations are tyrannical regimes of the worst kind, and states that engage in the mass slaughter of their citizens; the betrayal of such states would seem to merit praise rather than condemnation. Since ideologies are the criterion, and ideologies are different, there can be no agreement on what constitutes betrayal. Soviet agents who spied for communist tyrannies against democratic countries were motivated mostly by ideological reasons, at least in the early days of communism; it was not until later that money or blackmail, or both, took over from ideology. Are we to say, then, that such people – the Cambridge spy ring, for instance – were justified in what they did because their reasons were ideological? And if not, is it because their ideology was wrong or criminal? The difficulty is clear. Ideological motives often turn out to be nothing more than emotions; and if emotions could justify, then everything we did would be justified, and the concept of betrayal as something bad would lose its meaning.

And yet there is something unsatisfactory in merely pointing out the ambiguities involved in the concept of betrayal. We are not content to let the matter rest there because we feel that we need the concept of betrayal as an act that is by its very nature wrong; and because of its importance to us we feel that we should be able to define it absolutely, in clear and simple terms of right and wrong, not just relatively to some philosophy or political ideology.

For example: people who reveal to others things told to them in confidence, whether they do so for personal gain or for their own amusement, are clearly guilty of betrayal. Indeed, we say of such people that they have 'betrayed a confidence'. In cases such as these, where we are dealing with individuals, we find it fairly easy to decide whether or not someone has been betrayed. Even if an act of betrayal is forgiven, it nevertheless remains an act of betrayal: St Peter was forgiven by his lord and saviour for renouncing him in a time of danger, and yet was designated by him as his successor and the founder of the Church. The theological interpretations of this event need not, however, concern us here.

Political betrayal, or treason, is a more ambiguous notion, for a variety of reasons. Firstly because right and wrong tend not to be clearly distinguishable in politics, and situations where they are clearcut, such as the Second World War, do not occur very often. Secondly because, as a result of this, we often have to distinguish between a greater and a lesser evil. Thus we are forced to conclude, for example, in spite of all that we know about communism and the results of the war, that people who worked for Soviet intelligence during the war were serving a good cause because they were working against the Germans, and at that time Nazi Germany was the worst evil and the greatest threat. And thirdly because people's motivations muddy the waters still further: people who betray an evil cause for personal gain, and not because it is an evil cause, do not deserve our respect; on the other hand, people who serve an evil cause for ideological reasons, and not for personal gain, are not justified either, if it is fairly clear that the cause really is an evil one. In short, there is no such thing as absolute good in politics, and there is nothing we can do about it. This in turn may lead us to suspect that there is also no such thing as absolute evil in politics; that, however, is more doubtful.

It is fairly certain, then, that people will often disagree about whether particular acts are acts of betrayal. But if we find it easier to deal with cases where the victim of betrayal is an individual and not a nation, a state or a church, this is because in such cases we know more or less what is important, and what to hold on to. If we know it, and hold on to it, then those cases where the victim of betrayal is a nation, a state, or a church will also become easier to deal with.

11
ON VIOLENCE

Violence is part of culture, not nature. When a bird swallows an insect, or a wolf savages a deer, we do not say that these are acts of violence. Nor, unless we are animal rights fanatics, would we say that boiling prawns is an act of violence. We use the word 'violence' only in relation to people; only people can do, and suffer, violence. To commit an act of violence is to use force or the threat of force to make people behave in a certain way, or to prevent them from doing certain things, or just to do them harm for the sake of it.

Most of us also distinguish between the justified and the unjustified use of force: institutions of the state, for instance, such as the police, the courts and the legal system, are justified in their use of force in order to prevent or punish certain types of behaviour that we consider criminal. There are people, however, who condemn all forms of violence, including the use of force by the state, although it is hard to imagine a world in which nothing was punishable by law. People who believe that violence in any form is wrong sometimes try to justify their belief by appealing to the Sermon on the Mount, in which Jesus told us not to oppose evil, but to turn the other cheek. Jesus, however, was talking only about individuals, and how they should behave when subjected to violence by others: by his own example, his own martyrdom and death, he showed us that we can refuse to return violence for violence, not through fear but through faith and spiritual strength, and yet conquer the world. He was not talking about the mechanisms of the state, and he left no political doctrine; he was convinced that the end of the world was imminent, although, on his own admission, he did not know when it would come. However, he himself resorted to violence when he chased the moneylenders out of the temple.

Violence has been an ineradicable part of human history from its very beginnings. So has war, which is simply an organized form of collective violence. It does not follow that war and violence should be considered a good thing; nevertheless, there have been plenty of people who thought it not only a natural but indeed a useful part of life, seeing it as an opportunity for instilling the manly virtues, such as courage and the spirit of sacrifice for one's tribe. To them, war was the best way of developing nobility of spirit, heroism and endurance in the young. Now courage is undeniably a good thing, but these people argued that war was a good thing because it provided us with the opportunity to develop precisely those virtues which are useful in time of war. In other words, they were assuming not only that there always have been wars, but that there always will be.

Since it is a fairly safe bet that violence in its various forms will continue to be a constant part of our lot, it is possible that wars, too, will go on being waged. There are good reasons for thinking that wars will indeed continue. They include not only the existence of old tribal enmities but also the development of genuine conflicts, concerning, for example, access to water or farmland or, when population density starts to become intolerable, to territory of any kind. But the glorification of war for its own sake must surely seem incomprehensible to the great majority of those who lived through the Second World War and all its horrors. Pierre Proudhon and, later, Georges Sorel could still praise war, but when people from later generations, like Ernst Jünger, did so it was the First World War they were thinking of.

Today one rarely hears war praised for its own sake; the endless tribal massacres in Africa and the horrors of Bosnia supply scant arguments for the charm of the martial arts. And it is significant that of the countless wars, great and small, that took place in almost every corner of the earth after the end of the First World War, not one was waged between democratic countries; for wars are born of tyranny. The world's democracies doubtless had plenty of sins on their conscience, and have been known to resort to force in their politics of empire; but they did not wage war against one another. Instead, they created mechanisms which allowed them to solve their conflicts through negotiation and compromise; and while these sometimes included blackmail and deceit, they did not include wholesale slaughter. There are good reasons for our stereotyping of the conflict between Athens and Sparta: our culture really came from Athens, which educated its youth (the citizens, of course, not the slaves) in poetry, philosophy and art, and not from Sparta, where military skills dominated the curriculum – although Athens, too, practised the politics of empire. Violence may be an inevitable part of our lives, and we must always expect it; but there is no reason to lacedaemonize – in other words, to think like the Spartans – or see it as anything other than an unfortunate necessity.

It seems fairly simple, in theory, to distinguish between justified and unjustified violence or, to take a particular instance of this distinction, between a defensive and an offensive war; but in reality few situations are so clear-cut. In the twentieth century, of course, there have been only 'victims of aggression': no country likes to call itself an aggressor, even if its act of aggression has an ideological basis, as in the cases of Nazi Germany (the need for 'Lebensraum' for the master race) and the Soviet

Union (the Leninist principle that war is always justified if it is waged by a socialist state, which is the embodiment of the 'progressive class'; the question of who started it is irrelevant). In some cases it is easy to identify the aggressor: Germany in 1939, Japan in 1941, the Soviet Union in 1939 and again in 1956 in Hungary, and North Korea in 1950. Other cases are much less clear; deciding 'who started it' can be as difficult as sorting out a scuffle in a children's playground ('He pushed me!' – 'But he kicked me!' – 'But he pushed me first!' – 'That's because he called me a pig!' – 'That's not true, he called me names first!' – and so on).

So the distinction between justified and unjustified violence, although clear enough in many particular instances, is not so easy to define. The corporal punishment of children as a regular part of their upbringing is doubtless an instance of unnecessary violence, but we would not describe as violence the various physical constraints we impose on small children in order to prevent them from hurting themselves. And what about indoctrination? Is it violence to impose our beliefs on children, who do not have the mental powers to resist? When we initiate children into our culture, we indoctrinate them; that is unavoidable. Should we say, then, that indoctrination can take two forms, good and bad, and that only the second of these should be described as violence? But if we distinguish between good and bad indoctrination on the basis of what we consider to be the right beliefs, principles and norms, then our definition of violence will be based on our own view of the world; and that surely will not do.

Can non-physical coercion in general be described as 'moral violence'? Blackmail is clearly an instance of violence; a hunger strike, intended perhaps to force concessions of some kind from a government, is a less obvious case. If it is used to protest against inhuman prison conditions, we would probably consider it justified, since it is the only form of protest available to a prisoner; but if it is used as an attempt to force political concessions from a democratic government, we would probably call it a form of violence.

It seems clear that in order to distinguish between justified and unjustified violence we must be able to evaluate the ends for which it is used. Where the end is unquestionably a worthy one, violence can be considered justified (albeit not always prudent), *provided* that there is no other way of attaining that end. A tyranny, for example, can only be fought with violence, and even Christian theologians have argued that the killing of a tyrant is justified. In totalitarian countries we have witnessed a struggle that was successful despite being non-violent, but it took place at a time when totalitarianism was already considerably weakened; when it was strong and could be ruthless with impunity, non-violent struggle had no chance of succeeding, for the regime had the means to stifle any attempt at disobedience at its earliest stage and prevent news of it from spreading.

The end that is to justify the use of violence must be specific, well-circumscribed and clearly defined: winning independence for a country subjugated by another power, killing a despot, punishing a criminal. The 1960s youth movement whose participants resorted to what they called 'revolutionary' violence in order to build an 'alternative society' (of precisely what kind they were unable to say, but to them this was a matter of pride rather than concern) had no justification whatsoever, and neither did their teachers, foremost among them Sartre and Marcuse; they simply entertained deluded visions of destroying democratic institutions and establishing their own tyranny. Fortunately they were unsuccessful. But during the same period others, in communist countries, were fighting tyranny with only the word as their weapon: all the violence was on the side of the regime. In the end their struggle proved successful, in that it slowly changed the way people thought, showed them that fear could be conquered, and exposed the lies and lawlessness of the regime. In their case the use of some forms of violence would have been justified, although probably ineffective.

It is easy for us to say that we want a world without

violence, but no one has yet come up with a sensible recipe for such a world. To condemn all forms of violence absolutely and indiscriminately is to condemn life. But a world in which violence is directed only against crime, slavery, aggression and tyranny is not an irrational thing to strive for – not even if we have plenty of good reasons for doubting the likelihood of such an outcome.

12
ON BOREDOM

I shall try not to be boring about boredom. In other words, I shall try to be brief. The problem of boredom is in itself neither boring nor trivial, for it concerns a sensation we have all experienced. It is not a pleasant - sensation, but it cannot, except in extreme cases (psychological experiments involving sense-deprivation, for instance), be called suffering.

Boredom, like aesthetic qualities, can be both experienced and attributed to the thing experienced: I can be bored by a novel, but the novel itself can also be boring. It is therefore an appropriate subject for what some people like to call 'phenomenological' study.

When we consider the everyday usage of the word, the first thing we notice is that we attribute boredom only to things that we experience in time. Thus a play, a concert, a historical treatise and work can all be boring. But we wouldn't normally say that a painting was boring, for a painting is a thing we usually take in at a glance. A landscape can be boring if looked at for a long time: a snow-covered plain viewed from a train window, for example, can become boring because of its monotony and absence of contrasts. The things we experience can be boring either because they are repetitive or because they are chaotic, meaningless or disjointed (although a novel or a play that depicts a chaotic or disjointed world need not be boring: Beckett and Joyce are good examples); and we are bored when our experience of those things is so changeless and monotonous, so lacking in the promise of novelty, that we feel we are in a world where nothing new ever happens or can be expected to happen, and if it does we do not care: as far as we are concerned it might not have happened at all.

One could argue that nothing is boring in and of itself, for people vary widely in their response to different bits of the world, and are bored, or not, according to their past experiences and present circumstances. A film we once found interesting becomes boring when seen again soon afterwards, because what happens in it has already happened for us. Someone who knows little about music might be bored by certain symphonies of Brahms but not by, say, the violin concertos of Tchaikovsky or Paganini or the piano concertos of Chopin, while the more musically knowledgeable would disagree and condemn such a person's response as ignorant. A historical treatise that others found fascinating might bore me to tears because

I had no familiarity or associations with the subject, and thus could not perceive contrasts or distinguish what was important or original in it from what was not. A job that seems boring to someone who has been doing it routinely for a long time need not necessarily bore a beginner; an Agatha Christie murder mystery would be extremely boring if we tried to read it in a language we did not know. And so on.

It seems clear that boredom, or boringness, depends to a great degree on our own experiences and individual responses to the world, and that there can be no unanimity about it. To ask whether something can be boring in and of itself is therefore rather like asking whether aesthetic qualities are always merely projections of our individual responses, or inherent in some way in the object of our perceptions, the 'thing itself'. There are certainly areas of agreement and of disagreement in both cases; and in both cases the qualities under discussion are culture-dependent. But it may be that the question is simply unanswerable: that when we perceive these qualities, mind and object act upon one another, and this reciprocal influence between our perceptions and the object perceived makes it impossible to say, or even to ask, which came first.

We think of boredom not only as a universal human phenomenon – a feeling that affects us all rather than a privilege restricted to, say, Baudelaire or Chateaubriand

– but also as a uniquely human one. We do not think of animals as creatures that feel boredom. If there is no danger and their physical needs have been satisfied, they lie about doing nothing, conserving their energy, and there is no reason to think that they are bored. (And if dogs get bored, as we sometimes imagine they do, it is probably because they learnt it from us.) Nor is it clear when humans first began to articulate their experience of boredom; it does not seem to have been a subject of literary or philosophical texts before the nineteenth century, even though the word itself existed. Did peasants, in their traditional primitive villages, become bored with the sameness of their daily round, with toiling away from dawn to dusk just to survive, and staying always in the same place? We have no way of knowing, but we may suppose that even a lot such as theirs, with no prospect of change, almost outside time, need not have induced a constant feeling of boredom. There was always something out of the ordinary going on: children being born, children dying, neighbours committing adultery, droughts and thunderstorms, fires and floods. All these things, unexpected and mysterious, dangerous or benign, must have relieved the monotony of their existence, and made them feel that their lives were in the grip of unpredictable whims of fate.

The normality and monotony of the everyday can indeed seem boring. We often complain that the news the mass media choose to print or broadcast is always bad: nothing but droughts and famines, wars and crises, murders and mass slaughter. Just as often, people will reply that this is because only bad news is news. If Mr Smith gets killed in the street, that's news; but if Mr Smith gets up, eats breakfast, goes to work and comes home again, that's not news: it's boring. If Mr Jones gets divorced, that's news (at least for his friends); but if he lives in blissful harmony with his wife, that's not news, it's boring. News is made up of the improbable and the unpredictable, and what is unpredictable also tends to be unfavourable to us; the chaos of the world is not for us to benefit from. The history of humanity is one long struggle with unpredictability and chance; but if chance were on the whole favourable to us, we would have no reason to want to reduce its influence on our lives. It is true that Mr Smith's winning the lottery is also news, despite being good news; but it is good news only for Mr Smith, and not for the rest of us who bought a ticket and lost, thus allowing Mr Smith to win. So even Mr Smith's winning the lottery turns out, on the whole, to be bad news after all.

Those of us who are lucky enough to spend the greater part of their lives reading books, to take one example, generally do not become bored, in the sense that they are never at a loss for things to stimulate their interest; for them, such things are always within arm's reach. Indeed, one might wonder how anyone could ever be bored in a world with constant access to radio, television, music and other forms of entertainment, where it is surely easy enough to find something to hold one's interest. And yet we are constantly hearing and reading about gangs of violent youths marauding through the world's cities gratuitously destroying or assaulting anything or anyone in their path, and explaining their behaviour by saying that they are bored. It seems that watching exciting films is not enough – perhaps because watching films is a passive occupation, in which we are unable to forget that what we are watching is fiction, or to feel that we are really participating in the action. Indeed, even the most exciting adventures of television heroes can increase our boredom and our hunger for some kind of stimulation, and even give rise to feelings of injustice: 'Why isn't my life as interesting as that detective's? Why don't I have as much money as Elizabeth Taylor? It's not fair.' What is to be done with these poor young people, who have food in their mouths and clothes on their backs, but no riches and no real or fictional adventures of the kind they imagine film stars to have? It is easy to say that we must channel their curiosity and their need for stimuli into something 'constructive', so that they do not express themselves in gratuitous destruction or collective ecstasy at concerts of meaningless and deafening noise; but how?

Curiosity, like boredom, is a uniquely human quality – the human quality *par excellence*. It is curiosity that spurs us on to explore the world even after we have satisfied our physical needs and made sure that no dangers threaten us. It is, in other words, the quality that above all others takes us beyond the animal state. Like boredom and the quality of being boring, curiosity and the quality of being interesting – i.e. an object of curiosity – can be attributed respectively to our experience of objects and to the objects themselves; the one cannot exist without the other. And since 'being curious' and 'being interesting' are opposites and complements of 'being bored' and 'being boring' respectively, one might say that boredom is the price we pay for curiosity: if we were never bored, we would never be curious. In other words, our capacity to be bored is an essential part of our humanity; we are human because we can be bored.

The feeling of boredom is naturally something we want to escape, and our attempts to escape it can take both destructive and constructive forms. The former, however, is easier. War, for example, is a dreadful thing, but it is not boring; the eagerness to fight, and the instincts aroused in battle, are good antidotes to boredom, and must have been among the causes of many wars. Moreover, since boredom is often caused by repetitiveness, it is more than likely that one by one our existing sources of interest will be exhausted, and we shall need ever more and stronger stimuli, like drug addicts. There is no telling what such a situation may lead to.

One particular instance of the phenomenon we have been considering is the 'boring person'. The boring person is extraordinarily difficult to describe. His boringness has nothing to do with his education or lack of it, or with his character. He need not be someone who constantly repeats himself; more often the boring person tends to be someone who cannot distinguish between the important and the unimportant. His anecdotes are full of needless and cumbersome detail; he is a stranger to both humour and irony; he will harp on a subject long after everyone else has lost interest. In short, he seems to lack the normal mechanisms of human interaction. Perhaps this is precisely because he is unable to create the necessary contrasts in human communication. If so, he would fit the general description of boredom I have outlined.

That state of perfect satisfaction, without conflicts or stress, which we call utopia, would surely, if it were ever to come about, spell the end of humanity; for in it our instinct for curiosity would wither. This is why, while our species is what it is, utopia can never be built. But can we not imagine an 'end of history' as recently foretold by Francis Fukuyama, namely a world without any conceivable alternatives to existing political institutions, without wars and poverty, art or literature – a world, in short, of general and unremitting boredom? The prospect is too unlikely to cause us any serious worry, but if it did come about, we would all rapidly find ourselves not so much resigned to lives of boredom as desperately searching for precisely the kind of solution adopted by marauding inner-city gangs: the impulse to destroy just for the sake of it. This is why boredom, like all universal human phenomena, can be both beneficial and dangerous.

13

ON FREEDOM

There are two large areas of thought which deal with the question of freedom. They are distinct and logically independent of one another, indeed to such an extent that one might be forgiven for doubting that they do in fact deal with the same thing. The first is that current in human thought which from time immemorial has battled with the problem of man's freedom as a human being. This current has been concerned with the question of whether man is free by virtue of his humanity alone, in other words with free will and freedom of choice. The second is concerned with man's freedom as a member of society, and deals with the social freedom of action which we also call liberty.

When we say that man is free by virtue of the very nature of his humanity, we mean among other things that he is capable of choice, and that his choices are not entirely dependent on, or inevitably caused by, forces beyond his consciousness. Freedom, however, is not just the ability to choose between possibilities that are already given; it is also the capacity to create situations that are quite new and quite unpredictable.

Throughout the history of our culture man's freedom in this sense has been denied as often as it has been affirmed. The debate is related, although not identical, to the debate concerning general determinism. If every event is wholly determined by the sum of its conditions, then the possibility of free choice does not even arise. But if universal causality were really so inexorable, it might lead to some rather paradoxical results. For if something is entirely determined by its conditions it is also, in principle (although not necessarily in practice), predictable; so if strict determinism were true, we could imagine, once our powers of prediction were sufficiently perfected, opening our morning paper and reading an announcement like the following: 'John Green, the famous composer, was born last night in Twickenham. Tomorrow the London Philharmonic will commemorate this event by playing his Third Symphony, which he will compose at the age of 37.'

There was a time when physicists, and most philosophers, believed in strict determinism; when it was an essential foundation of scientific and rational thought. There were no proofs to support it, but it was considered a matter of plain common sense, a truth so self-evident that only a madman could doubt it. In our century quantum mechanics and, more recently, chaos theory have done much to undermine this belief, and physicists have abandoned the dogma of determinism. The discoveries of quantum mechanics do not, of course, entail that man has free will – electrons, after all, do not have free will – but at least physics has not rendered our belief in free will ridiculous or irrational. And indeed it is neither of these things. We not only may but *should* believe in free will, in the sense in which I have defined it above: as a capacity not only to choose but to create new possibilities. The experience of freedom in this sense is so basic for every human being that its reality seems irresistibly evident although we cannot prove it by taking it apart and analysing its constituent elements. But the fact that it is so basic as to seem compellingly obvious is no reason to doubt that it is real. We really are free agents in what we do, not merely instruments of the various forces that exist in the world – although we are, of course, subject to the laws of nature. And we really do set ourselves goals, good or bad, and strive to achieve them. External conditions or other people may undermine our efforts – we may, for instance, be so physically incapacitated as to be effectively incapable of making choices – but our essential capacity to choose is still there, even though we may not be able to take advantage of it. Nor is there any reason to claim, like St Augustine or Kant, that we are free only when we choose good, not when we choose evil; to say this is to define our freedom not by our very capacity to choose but by the content of our choices, and to define freedom in this way is to encumber the very concept of freedom with our own moral doctrines.

This freedom, then, is given to us along with our humanity, and is the foundation of that humanity; it gives uniqueness to our very existence.

The second of the two areas of thought about freedom deals with a very different question, for its subject is our freedom not as human beings but as members of society. Freedom in this sense is derived not from the nature of our existence but from our culture, society and laws. It denotes that area of human activity in which social organization neither forbids nor dictates, but leaves us free to choose how we act without fear of reprisals. This is the freedom which we also call liberty.

Freedom in this sense is of course measurable in degrees: there can be more or less of it, and we generally evaluate different political systems according to the degree of freedom they afford. The scale stretches from perfect totalitarian regimes (such as Stalinist Russia, Maoist China and other varieties of Asian communism, or the Third Reich) at one extreme to political systems in which government intervention in the form of prohibitions or injunctions is limited to a strict minimum. Totalitarian regimes aim to regulate every sphere of human activity so that nothing is left to individual choice. Tyrannies of a non-totalitarian variety aim to suppress freedom in areas where it might represent a threat to the regime, but in other matters they do not aim for total control. They also need not have any kind of global or all-encompassing ideology.

It is not difficult to see that freedom in this sense, although it can be reduced to zero, cannot be unlimited. The hypothetical 'state of nature' discussed by social theorists, a state without laws or rules or any kind of organized society, with everyone constantly at war with everyone else, has never existed; but if it did exist, it would not be a state of unlimited freedom. It would not be true to say that in such a state 'everything is permissible', because something can be permissible or not only by law, and where there are no laws there is no freedom: the word simply loses its meaning. Freedom, in our world, is always circumscribed. Robinson Crusoe did not enjoy unlimited freedom, indeed he enjoyed no freedom of any sort. Freedom, in greater or lesser degree, can exist only where something is forbidden while something else is permitted.

Perhaps the following joke, which must date from before the First World War, can make things clearer: 'In Austria, whatever is not forbidden is permitted; in Germany, whatever is not permitted is forbidden; in France, everything is permitted, including whatever is forbidden; and in Russia, everything is forbidden, including whatever is permitted.'

Although these two meanings of the word 'freedom' are very different, so much so that it is possible to enjoy freedom in one sense but not in the other, nevertheless they are close enough for us to be able to use the same word for both, as long as we do not confuse them. Both have to do with the possibility of choice: 'freedom' in the first sense is our very ability as human beings to choose and create, although the fact that we have this ability presupposes nothing about the range of choices that are in fact open to us; in the second sense it is the area in which society and the law leave us free to make our own choices.

There are two frequent errors one should beware of when talking about freedom. The first is to confuse freedom with the satisfaction of all our desires and what we consider to be our rightful claims. There is nothing wrong with talking about being 'free from pain' or 'free from hunger', and not to suffer pain or hunger is indeed one of the most basic of human claims; nevertheless, we cannot be said to enjoy some peculiar sort of freedom when these claims are fulfilled. The use of the word 'freedom' is misleading here because it has nothing to do with choice; it is neither about the extent of our freedom to choose nor about our ability to choose and create. Pain is just something we are glad to get rid of; it stops, and that's that. To be rid of pain is a good that is highly desirable; so is an apple to someone who is hungry or sleep to someone who is tired, or anything at all that we happen to desire at any particular moment. But getting rid of pain or eating an apple is not a variety of freedom; it is simply a desired good. (We can imagine a concentration camp in which there is no hunger; would we say that it provides certain freedoms to the prisoners, while a liberal democracy provides others?) So many people in our century, and in centuries past, have given their lives fighting for freedom in the proper sense of the word that to extend its meaning to include anything anyone might ever want is to blur our grasp of the concept itself and leave the word without any meaning at all; the root of the concept is gnawed away. The distinction between 'freedom from' and 'freedom to' is needless.

The second error we should beware of in talking about freedom is to assume that freedom in the second, legal sense, is meaningless if our other needs or desires are not fulfilled. This was an assumption frequently made by communists: 'What does political freedom matter,' they would ask, 'to someone who is hungry and unemployed?' Well, it does matter. Hunger may be more urgently felt than the lack of political freedoms, but when these freedoms are present the hungry and unemployed have a far better chance of improving their lot than when they are absent: they can organize themselves to fight for their rights and protect their interests.

While including all the goods we might desire under the heading of 'freedom' is inappropriate, there is no doubt that freedom in the legal sense is itself a good that is highly desirable. Moreover, it is a good in itself, and not merely as an instrument or condition of obtaining other goods. This does not mean, however, that we may accept without restriction the principle that the more freedom (in this sense), the better. Most of us probably feel it is a good thing that certain activities which used to be regarded as crimes, like witchcraft or homosexuality, are no longer regarded as such, at least in civilized countries. But no one in his right mind would demand the right to drive on the right or the left hand side of the road as it happens to suit him. More and more often, and in an increasing number of countries, one hears that school-children have too much freedom and not enough discipline, and that not only their academic but also their moral and civic education suffer as a result. Nor is it at all certain that children want to be given the greatest possible measure of freedom from an early age; the desire naturally increases with age, but small children tend to accept the authority of adults quite naturally and generally do not demand to be allowed to choose for themselves. Similarly, we ourselves, as adults, are often relieved to be able to leave certain choices to others, especially when we are not sure of ourselves and would prefer to act on the advice of an expert – even though we know that not all experts can be trusted. We know that making the right choice often depends on having the right information, and no one can claim to be sufficiently knowledgeable in every sphere in which he is called upon to make choices. We have the freedom to choose, but we prefer not to avail ourselves of it in matters with which we are unfamiliar.

In short, there is no general rule we could use to determine exactly how much freedom is good for us. Sometimes we are right in thinking that we can have too much freedom rather than not enough, and that freedom beyond certain limits can be harmful. Excess is no doubt safer than insufficiency in this respect, and it may be more prudent for the law to err on the side of liberality rather than caution in the measure of freedom it accords to citizens; but even this principle cannot be accepted without restriction.

14
ON LUXURY

We sometimes have occasion to use the word 'luxury', and its meaning seems clear to us; we know what we mean by phrases such as 'Those people live in luxury and are indifferent to the poverty of others'; 'I can't afford such a luxurious car'; 'luxury is sinful but pleasant'. But when we try to define the meaning of the word, we soon find ourselves bogged down in what seems an impossible task. We are tempted to begin by saying that luxury is something people want but do not actually need: something nice that we can nevertheless live without. But we can also live without art, music, literature or wine, and yet we would not say that these things are luxuries. We take countless devices of modern technology for granted: it would not occur to us to say that cars, electricity or television sets are luxuries. Yet we know that for centuries people lived without these things, and therefore that they are not necessities of life. People also lived without reading, writing or metal instruments, but we would not say that these are things we do not 'really' need. Since the only thing really essential for our survival is the satisfaction of our physical needs, we could say that anything beyond that qualifies as luxury; abolishing luxury would then mean going back to the Stone Age. Few of us would rejoice in such a prospect.

Each of us doubtless has vague ideas of his own about how luxury, as something reprehensible, should be defined, and they probably sound something like this: 'Luxury is a thing I don't desire, but others do. The things I desire are "real" needs, but anything beyond that is not a real need.' It quickly becomes clear, however, that the distinction between people's needs and their desires is an arbitrary one, perhaps even frivolous. Let us suppose that I have one car; it is a small, fairly modest car, but I don't feel I need a bigger or better one. What right do I have to declare that someone who has (or would like to have) three cars does not really need them? On what grounds, and by what conceivable criteria, could I determine this? Would I say that wanting three cars is just a whim, an imagined need?

Perhaps we should just say that whatever we desire is a real need for us. After all, humanity has evolved precisely by creating new needs and new ways of satisfying them. Since all these needs are part of culture, not nature, a 'back to nature' ideology might dismiss them as 'artificial', but few of us accept such a judgement. People have lived without cars and refrigerators, but now that these useful objects have become easily available we can hardly imagine life without them.

Should we, then, abandon the concept of luxury as useless and meaningless? Not necessarily: perhaps we should first look for other, more intuitive criteria by which luxury could be defined. Some things which were once considered luxurious have become generally available, at least in relatively rich parts of the globe, while others have not. It is just not possible for everyone to have a château on the Loire. One could, theoretically, have a bolshevik or anarchist revolution and dispossess the owners of the châteaux, but the only result of this would be that the châteaux, instead of belonging to the aristocracy, would belong to party secretaries – a poor return, surely, for the millions of corpses which such a revolution would inevitably produce. We are naturally shocked when we see islands of luxury amid great poverty; but although we must do our best to fight hunger and want, and improve the lives of the poor, there is no point in fighting luxury, however we define it. To fight for the abolishment of luxury as an end in itself is to be guided not by some noble ideal of justice but by envy.

How, then, should we go about trying to define luxury – assuming that our aim is not its abolition through the dispossession of the rich, but a purely intellectual kind of profit? Let us consider the watch. When all watches were of the mechanical, wind-up variety, watches made by Patek-Philippe cost a fortune and were considered to be the most precise and reliable in the world. Today a Swatch which costs perhaps twenty-five dollars is probably just as precise as a Patek-Philippe, but Pateks still cost a fortune and still find plenty of buyers. Why do people buy them? To show others how rich they are? Or as a constant reminder of it to themselves? It is clear, at any rate, that what was once considered to be the chief virtue of a watch, namely its reliability, seems to have become, in the case of Pateks, quite beside the point; the function of a watch is no longer to tell the time, but something quite different. There are plenty of other such examples. A Rolls Royce is doubtless in many respects a better car than a humble Ford, but is it really ten times better, given that it costs roughly ten times as much? It is possible that, with the progress of technology, each of us will soon be able to own a reproduction of a Vermeer or a Van Gogh that will be visually indistinguishable from the original. But from time to time real Van Goghs will come up for auction, and there will always be people prepared to spend millions in order to own them. From simple snobbery? Perhaps. But most of us would prefer the real thing to an imitation, however perfect; there is undoubtedly a certain kind of satisfaction to be derived from owning something we know to be unique. Is this kind of satisfaction necessarily reprehensible?

There are, as we know, no limits to human needs and human greed. This being so, it is unlikely that we could ever arrive at an 'objective' and universally valid definition of 'luxury'. For what is or is not considered to be a luxury is always defined within the context of a particular civilization, historical conditions, country or social class. Nor should we forget that greed, although morally reprehensible and responsible for most crimes, is nevertheless also responsible (along with sloth) for some of the most brilliant achievements of the human spirit of technological invention, which has led to our lives becoming easier, more comfortable, and more luxurious (in a neutral sense); while attempts to eradicate greed by institutional means have led only to immeasurable suffering and poverty. Whatever is morally bad need not also be bad in all other respects; we may find this an uncomfortable thought to live with, but philosophers, including Hegel and Leibniz, have always known it to be true. Even theologians have discoursed on the unintended blessed effects of original sin. Calvinists condemned luxury as a way of life and wanted to reduce as much as possible the difference between rich and poor as it was expressed in everyday life, but they did not condemn the amassing of riches. On the contrary, they encouraged it – thus encouraging greed. Catholics condemned greed in theory, but they did not condemn luxury as such, and indeed papal courts have provided us with some splendid examples of it. Nor are Jesus's words concerning the camel, the rich man and the eye of the needle often quoted today as a precept for us to live by.

If, in spite of this, we still insist that luxury is always reprehensible, other distinctions are needed. Let us go back to watches. Patek watches are beyond the means of most people, but they do not proclaim their price in a crude or vulgar way. They are not ostentatious; they would not appeal to those who like to flaunt their wealth. In short, they are elegant; and elegance, though it may not be easy to define, is not reprehensible. It is best defined by examples: an elegant woman prefers moderation to ostentation; a woman hung about with jewels like a Christmas tree is not elegant. An elegant writer is one who can express himself clearly and concisely, pare his text down to its essentials and make the reader feel that its form is perfectly suited to its content. Moderation seems to be an essential element of elegance. An elegant woman, an elegant football match, an elegant dinner, an elegant piece of writing, an elegant architectural construction, and an elegant mathematical proof all have this in common, that they display moderation: it is their simplicity and lack of ostentation that lends them harmony and grace. Elegance and grace are forms of politeness, distinctive and easily recognized, while crudeness and vulgarity are expressive of efforts to achieve distinction by flaunting one's own wealth and superiority over others.

Thus luxury as something reprehensible does not consist in 'unnecessary' pleasures or satisfactions, because there can be no universal definition of what is unnecessary. Rather, it is an expression of the desire to flaunt one's wealth in a display of ostentation, and can provoke envy or derision, depending on the observer.

15
ON GOD

When we talk about God we do not know who or what we are talking about. We do it easily because centuries of such talk have forged a way of speaking which has become an entrenched part of our culture; but a moment's reflection is enough to make us realize with dismay that, in spite of this, we do not really know who or what we are talking about.

Our greatest difficulty is this: the God of the Bible upbraids our primogenitors in the Garden of Eden, gives orders to Noah, makes a covenant with Abraham, and speaks to Moses. When He does these things He speaks as a master, a ruler, a king. But the theologians tell us, supposedly from an analysis of that same Bible, that God is a timeless Being; that He is infinite, omniscient and all-powerful; that He knows all things through Himself, never going outside Himself, for *He is all being*, and all existence is contained in Him.

All this is easy to say, because we are used to it; but we

do not really understand what it means. We do not know what it means to exist outside time, to contain all past and future within one's eternal present. We do not know what it means to be all-powerful, and indeed the theologians themselves have disagreed on this point (the Greek *pantokrator*, which suggests a ruler or master of everything, is easier to understand than its Latin equivalent, *omnipotens*). We do not know what it means to create the world from nothing. Nor do we know what it means to be omniscient and omnipresent, or what the Holy Trinity is, or what the identity of essence and existence could be.

It is true that an acknowledgement of mystery has always been a tenet of Christian teaching; indeed the canons of the First Vatican Council prescribe excommunication for anyone who says that Revelation contains no mysteries in the proper sense, and that all the dogmas of the faith can be grasped and proven through reason. It is also true that our minds encounter far more mysteries than are talked of by theologians or in Scripture; we have only to think a little to see how the apparently simplest things and events encountered in our daily lives can awaken a feeling of fathomless mystery: time, freedom, existence, space, cause, consciousness, matter, number, love, 'I', death. But the difference between these two kinds of mystery is that the mysteriousness inherent in the everyday can elude us entirely: we may very well disregard the mystery and restrict ourselves to using these concepts in their everyday sense, or even decide that they contain no mystery at all because the chemists and physicists have explained it away. And while we may talk of God in a similar way, without enquiring too closely or thinking about it too much, the mystery here is on the surface, immediately apparent. In addition, a believer may at any moment be asked, 'How do you know that God exists?', and must give some sort of answer, while 'What is time?' is a question that seldom crops up in ordinary conversation, and when it does a confession of ignorance is neither shameful nor embarrassing.

And yet this is the most cruelly baffling of mysteries, for how can the Absolute also be a *person* – infinitely higher, greater and better than us, but a person nonetheless, in the same sense as each one of us? Can we imagine Parmenides' Being, motionless in its self-identity, giving Noah precise instructions about the building of the Ark? Can we conceive of Plotinus's timeless One explaining things to Job, telling people not to charge interest on loans, not to eat hares or crabs, not to yoke an ass and an ox together to the plough? When we think about it, we are tempted, like some Gnostics, to distinguish the Old Testament *Jahveh* from the true, loving God, or, like Meister Eckhart, to separate the person-God from the nameless and bottomless depths of Godhood.

Christianity smoothes the way and alleviates some of

the discomfort through the two-natured person of Jesus Christ, the mediator. He is the Christians' true God: his name, unlike that of the Father, is known to us, as is his life, and no one surely doubts that he really walked the earth, prayed to his Father in heaven and spread his teaching among the people. Admittedly, God's incarnation, the divine filiation and the Holy Trinity are among the most enigmatic tenets of the doctrinal corpus of Christianity, but the Christ we know from the Gospels allows us to forget about theological mysteries and complexities. He will not examine us on theology, for he loves us, with all our faults and in all our wretchedness, and wants only that we should love him, and pray to God the Father. The rest may be revealed to us on the other side, or perhaps not even there.

However, while theological complexities may fade away in the face of the Christ of the Gospels, the problem of God-the-Creator cannot be dismissed. It is hardly plausible, given the existence of atheists, to claim that we are all born with an 'idea' of God which we carry in our souls. It is, however, plausible to maintain that our reason naturally aspires to encompass the totality of being; and that our will for order and our need to make sense of existence lead us instinctively to seek that which is both the root and the keystone of existence, and gives it its meaning. Even atheists, Nietzsche among them, knew this: order and meaning come from God, and if God really is dead, then we delude ourselves in thinking that meaning can be saved. If God is dead, nothing remains but an indifferent void which engulfs and annihilates us. No trace remains of our lives and our labours; there is only the meaningless dance of protons and electrons. The universe wants nothing and cares for nothing; it strives towards no goal; it neither rewards nor punishes. Whoever says that there is no God and all is well deceives himself.

Thus while belief in God may be preserved through culture and expressed in an infinite variety of words and images, all marked by the uncertain nature of our temporal existence, God is not a transient product of random and changeable cultural circumstances: He is that place to which Reason, the Imagination and the Heart are persistently drawn. He is that which has no cause outside itself, and about which we cannot ask, 'Who created God?' or 'What is God for, and why does He exist?'

God, the provider of meaning, must be a person, but He is also an Absolute: here, again, is the unfathomable mystery, the unsolvable puzzle. But it is not the only one: He must also be the source and provider of Good. For centuries defenders of the faith argued that the evil and human suffering that have always existed in the world cannot be taken as evidence against God's goodness, for all that happens through our own will is an inevitable consequence of our freedom; it is that freedom, they insisted, which enables us to rebel against God and break all His commandments, but without which we would not be human. As for the suffering with which nature herself plagues us, they claimed that it is just punishment for our sins. Sceptics have always rejected this explanation as inadequate, since the distribution of natural suffering clearly has nothing to do with the distribution or weight of the sins we commit. Another kind of reasoning, however, was sometimes attempted: according to it, when God created the physical world He endowed it with certain laws or mechanisms which function automatically and regardless of moral considerations, and physical human suffering is just one consequence of these laws.

But – one might ask – could not God have created the world differently? To this one can only reply that if our world were not subject to any of the laws of physics, but consisted only of an infinite succession of miracles, brought about by God in order to protect us from suffering at every moment, then it would not *be* a material world in any real sense. But – one might further ask – could it not be subject to laws without harming us in any way? We cannot be sure of the answer to this, partly because we cannot imagine what such a world would be like. We may, however, venture to suppose that God is not omnipotent in the sense of being able to arrange all the elements of the world in any combination He pleases, so as to produce laws of nature that would watch over our happiness and well-being: it seems reasonable to assume that God, too, must pay a price for everything He does.

It is true that suffering can be cleansing; but not every kind of suffering, and not always, and not for everyone. Christianity teaches that all suffering has meaning, even if we cannot see it; we should therefore put our trust in God unreservedly and accept our fate without struggle and without despair, for we are powerless to change it. Blessed are those whose faith is so unwavering.

But perhaps God is simply evil? Perhaps it was Satan who created the world and now rules over it? There have been those who believed this; the preachers who left us detailed descriptions of hell seemed to believe it, although they did not say so. Yet there is Good in the world, although we do not have the tools to quantify it and compare its mass to the mass of evil and suffering. There is also love, and friendship, and charity; there is compassion and sacrifice and forgiveness. There is Beauty and Reason; there is art and literature, and music, and mathematics; there are extraordinary achievements of technology. And there is also the joy of existence. Good does exist, and it would not if an evil demiurge ruled the world. This is why, if the presence of Good and Evil in this world were to determine our belief in the existence or non-existence of God, and in His goodness, the Good in the world would constitute a much stronger argument for His goodness than evil and suffering for His being evil:

not because there is more Good than Evil but because, if He were evil, there would be no Good at all, only eternal fire in infernal gloom.

Suffering has always existed, but it seems only now to have become such an obvious and compelling argument against God. It is hard to say whether this is because there is more of it now than there was before. Perhaps we just feel it more: certainly we tend to feel, nowadays, that all suffering is unfair. This, however, is the result rather than the cause of our unbelief.

Perhaps, again, God is more like us: sometimes good and sometimes evil, yet never so evil as to consign sinners to eternal torment? The Bible provides some good arguments for this view. As for those fathomless depths of Godhood, which are better left unplumbed, the attributes of Good and Evil do not apply to them.

16

ON RESPECT FOR
NATURE

Respect, as Kant said, is not an emotion, like love, or friendship, or fascination. Nor is it a belief, an intellectual state or act. It lies somewhere between the two, in a class by itself. Emotions need not be justified, although we can frequently give reasons to explain them; beliefs, on the other hand, unless they are self-evident, do require justification. But can respect be justified, and if so what kind of reasons can we give for saying that something deserves our respect? If you tell me that all persons deserve respect, and I ask you why, what will you say? You might simply say it is just because they are persons, but in that case I will reply: so what? What does it mean to say that a person is a person? At which point you, my humanist interlocutor, may be at a loss for an answer.

Indeed, why should anything at all – God, persons, moral law, nature, art, truth – deserve our respect? God perhaps because He is eternal, and truth possibly for the same reason (not, of course, each and every true proposition – that would be asking too much – but Truth as an eternal quality of each individual truth). And persons probably because here, too, we believe (however hard it may be to sustain this belief in certain particular instances) that we all carry within ourselves a divine spark, and are fashioned, as the Scriptures tell us, in God's image. The idea of God is the source of our self-respect; without God, as Hegel said, we cannot truly respect ourselves. It is also our custom to respect the bodies of the dead, and perhaps this is because they retain traces of those who inhabited them. In the same way, we respect nature and life itself perhaps because we see in them the hand of the Creator. Why else would we extend our respect to certain social positions, such as those of king, pope or president, regardless of who holds them? For a long time kings as well as popes were believed to have ascended their thrones by divine right, and it may be that our respect for secular heads of state, whom no one could possibly imagine to be anointed by God, is a remnant of that old belief, long extinguished in its literal interpretation.

In short, it is the sacred that we respect, and this respect, a pale reflection of a more ancient reverence, is felt even among those by whom God and holiness have been forgotten. It is at any rate possible that this is so. We can retain the vestiges of a dead belief long after the death of the belief itself, unmindful of their origins. But although they can persist for a long time, they cannot do so for ever. The canons of our civilization, rooted in Christianity and the Bible, demand that we respect all persons. But a civilization dominated by the spirit of rationalism and scientism will not long be able to preserve a place for the sacred. It will come to accept the belief, although without expressing it in so many words, that a person is reducible to his function; it will accept, in other words, that each person is entirely replaceable. Such a civilization would signal the end of humanity as we know it. This threat is kept at bay for the moment only by the belief that the greatest good and the highest value in the world is pleasure.

But let us suppose that you want to continue the discussion. You may say: let us assume that our respect for the various works of Creation has its source in our respect for God; and let us assume further that God exists and is the Creator of the world. Why – you may ask – should we respect Him? To this there is only one answer: we do not respect God as some kind of metaphysical being, we respect Him as the source and provider of the sacred. But if you go on to ask why the sacred should deserve our respect, your question has no meaning, for respect and sanctity are a single substance; they are two sides of the same reality, like love and the person loved.

There is one area of uncertainty in these explanations, and that is the source of our respect for nature. According to the Bible, it was God's intention that man should be master of nature. This implies that man may avail himself for his own purposes of all that nature provides; and the fact that God granted us permission to feed upon animals as well as plants (albeit at the same time imposing upon the chosen people a vast array of complicated restrictions and taboos the point of which, in truth, remains a mystery) clearly confirms this intention.

And yet today we are constantly being told to respect nature, because our continued thoughtless devastation of it will ultimately bring about our own destruction. But such claims are an abuse of language. If we want to protect nature for the sake of our own health and well-being and that of future generations, all we need is a rational assessment of the costs and benefits involved; respect does not enter into it. Surely no one would want to claim that the destruction of nature is a matter of indifference if it is harmful to man. But it makes no sense to insist, like the ecological slogans that harangue us at every turn, that we must protect and respect nature for its own sake: it is humanity that we must respect. Nature alone, considered apart from the human costs and benefits of its preservation, deserves no respect. This is the biblical and Kantian view. A possible reply to it is that we must nevertheless inculcate the habit of respect for nature as an end in itself, for only in this way can we ensure that people treat nature properly from the point of view of human concerns; but this reply begs the question, for it fails to address the real issue.

It is absurd to say that we should respect 'all forms of life'; this would entail respecting the tuberculosis bacillus and the smallpox virus. But we are not made of pure spirit; we are living organisms, and we cannot live without destroying other forms of life.

One might object, however, that the prospect of an earth without elephants, gorillas or tigers is a bleak one, whether or not we derive any benefits from these strange friends or enemies of ours. This is true, but here, too, the question is still one of human benefits, even if those benefits are purely aesthetic: the pleasure we take in contemplating the beauty and variety of nature is a uniquely human privilege. And it is a pleasure not easily abandoned: we have resigned ourselves, because we cannot do otherwise, to the disappearance of countless millions of species, which we shall never see except as poor dead remnants dug up by archaeologists; but this is no reason to assent meekly to the extermination of those that remain, even if our motivation is a purely aesthetic one.

Respect for nature as a thing of value in itself is not deeply rooted in religions of biblical provenance; it is an element that can be dispensed with. It is present more strongly in Oriental religions, which proclaim the unity of all life on earth. There is something attractive and good in these beliefs, and it may be that there are things they can teach us. They are proof, at any rate, that respect for nature may be a religious precept.

It is sometimes said that nature's very variety is a good thing from the human point of view, since scientists are constantly discovering new and unexpected benefits from various species of plants and animals. It is also true that this prodigious diversity itself protects nature against destruction: life, as Teilhard de Chardin wrote, forces its way in wherever it can. But often we are happy just to gaze at the various wonders of nature without any thought of the human benefits, amazed at how it is just the way it should be and glad that we are a part of it, even though we so often find ourselves having to defend us against its indifferent and unthinking destructiveness. It is then that we seem to glimpse a trace of divinity in nature, although we have no idea of the true relation between this trace and nature's presumed Creator.

We should conclude, then, that although it would be difficult to find good arguments for respecting nature as an end in itself, there is nothing wrong or unreasonable about such respect. On the contrary, it may be that by extending our respect to nature we can gain a better understanding of our own humanity.

17

ON SUPERSTITION

Few of us are prepared to admit that we are super-stitious. Yet we have all been raised among the symbols, gestures and beliefs that make up superstition, and often we half-believe in their significance without acknowledg-ing it even to ourselves. I once heard an anecdote about Niels Bohr, one of the great physicists of the twentieth century, which is a good illustration of this – even if it is apocryphal. Bohr, according to this anecdote, had a horseshoe nailed over his door. One day a friend of his asked him what it was for, and he said, 'I'm told it brings you luck'. 'But surely,' exclaimed the friend, perplexed, 'surely you don't mean to say that you, a physicist, actu-ally believe in that kind of superstition?' 'Well, no, of course I don't actually *believe* in it,' Bohr is supposed to have replied; 'but I'm told it works even if you don't believe it.'

There is no general agreement as to how superstition is to be defined. The great Catholic theologian Karl

Rahner has defined it as aping reverence for God in a form which is unworthy of Him: this is what we do when we put our faith in formulas and rituals in the hope of obtaining divine aid or foreseeing the future. Superstition is a quasi-religious cult of powers which, whatever they may be, are not God.

The Church has condemned a large variety of superstitions or things that it considered to be superstitions. Foremost among these was astrology, because it encouraged the belief that both individual lives and great historical events depend not on God's will but on the blind forces of the stars, which somehow manage to be both natural and directed. More recently it has condemned as superstitious spiritual seances and all forms of attempted communication with the dead, and declared the various unexplained phenomena occurring within this sphere of activity to be the workings of the devil. Belief in the devil and his antics is not itself a superstition because it is attested in Scripture, but Scripture contains no instances of attested belief in any technical measures whereby we might converse with the dead. (Jesus conversing with Moses and Elijah is not such an instance.) The Church also condemns soothsaying and divination in all its (extremely abundant) varieties, because foretelling the future is an activity restricted to prophets, who speak not in their own voice but in God's. And Calvin simply says: when we are guided by the word of God, we have true religion; when we follow our own notions, we have superstition.

Thus in the world of Christian customs and beliefs the criteria for distinguishing superstition are fairly clear. From the rationalist or scientistic point of view, however, the label of superstition applies to all forms of religious belief: belief in God and eternal life, in the efficacy of the sacraments, in miracles and prophecies, in the divinity of Jesus – all these are superstitions. This is presumably because none of these beliefs is testable by the accepted methods of scientific inquiry. And even though scientific beliefs often change, the scientistic doctrine itself remains the same, unshaken and untouched by the mistakes of science. Yet there was a time when belief in meteors, or falling stars as they were called, was considered a superstition; acupuncture, the efficacy of which on a variety of medical disorders is surely no longer in doubt, although its mechanisms remain mysterious, was for a long time similarly regarded. All beliefs not in accordance with the dogma of general determinism were once dismissed as superstitions. And so on. Conversely, beliefs once considered scientifically well-founded are sometimes discarded, although this does not always lead to their being labelled as superstitions. For a long time calcium salts were thought effective in the treatment of tuberculosis; they turned out to be of no use whatsoever, but people must have had reasons for believing in their efficacy, although evidently they were not very good ones. But in science no reasons are absolutely compelling; everything is subject to revision.

According to the rules of rationalism, however, beliefs are judged to be well-founded or not according to how we came by them and how we can justify them. This is where problems arise. We don't know how we came by the belief that the number thirteen is unlucky; there has been plenty of speculation about it, probably no more well-founded than the belief itself but by the rationalist canon admissible for all that. We know that the belief is a prevalent one because the evidence of attempts to cheat fate is everywhere around us: in the number of buildings lacking a thirteenth floor, for example, or an apartment numbered thirteen. But if someone were to calculate that on the thirteenth of each month there are indeed more accidents and tragedies than on other days, sceptics would not be convinced of the evil powers of the number thirteen. They would claim that the causality works in the opposite direction: people are afraid of the number thirteen, and this makes them particularly nervous on those days, so that they cause more accidents. The point is that while certain events or mechanisms fit within our canon of knowledge and accord with accepted scientific belief, others do not. We generally believe the ancient historians when they describe events for which no other sources exist, but we do not believe them when the events they describe go beyond this canon. Thus while we may be perfectly prepared to believe Livy's account of the wars waged by Romulus, we refuse to credit that Mars was the twins' father or that, after being thrown into the Tiber, they were raised by a she-wolf. In the same way, accounts of miracles accomplished by saints are disbelieved because things like miracles, which happen through divine intervention, do not fit into the canon. Nor will sceptics be persuaded to credit tales of inexplicable sudden cures at Lourdes: it is impossible to explain anything by appealing to divine intervention, and any other explanation would be better, however improbable.

Nowadays we often hear this type of issue being raised with reference to so-called paranormal phenomena. The evidence for these is most frequently what we call anecdotal, and it is quite difficult to organize the technical means of observing them. The number of people who claim to have encountered ghosts is enormous, but one can hardly ask the ghosts to present themselves in ranks before a panel of experts who could guarantee suitable experimental conditions and controls. Here, too, the accepted canon comes into play: many people think they have seen ghosts, but since ghosts do not exist, these people can only have been deluded, or hallucinating, or seeing visions while half-asleep, or simply making it up. Other paranormal phenomena are similarly treated. Countless people think they have had other-worldly experiences, encountered higher spirits from the beyond, or compellingly felt the presence of God; they will not convince the sceptics, for they cannot make these experiences available to their scrutiny, but they are satisfied in their own minds: their faith needs no additional confirmation. Again, almost all of us have at one time or another had experiences which might suggest that some sort of telepathic communication was at work; but here too it would be difficult to organize a strictly controlled experiment, and in any case advocates of the rationalist canon would not be interested, since they know in advance that telepathy is impossible and no technical means exist which could make it work. If experiments with so-called Zener cards have produced a series of correct guesses where the probability of their occurring by chance was fantastically small, the sceptic will not bother to look into the matter, considering such an occurrence to be impossible; even under the strictest experimental conditions there is always the possibility of a flaw, and often the experiment cannot be reproduced.

There have, however, been rationalists, not of the fanatically hardened variety but with impeccable ideological credentials, who have displayed an interest in some of these curious phenomena. One such was Eysenck, who was both a hard rationalist and an excellent interpreter of statistical data.

Another much-discussed topic from the list of curious

phenomena is the ability to predict the future. Can such an ability exist, and what would a prediction about the future have to be like in order to count as a true prophecy? Genuine predictions about the future would have to fulfil three conditions. First, the events predicted must be unlikely and impossible to predict from normal circumstances. In other words, foretelling the death within six months of a certain statesman who is known to be suffering from cancer cannot count as a genuine prediction. Secondly, the events predicted must be clear, not veiled in the kind of vague metaphors that could be applied to just about anything, like the predictions of Nostradamus; and they cannot be matters of commonsense certainty, like, for instance, the pronouncements of those American soothsayers who predict with perfect seriousness that the next few months will bring further troubles in the Middle East. Finally, it must be possible to verify whether or not the events predicted came to pass, and of course the prophecy cannot be a self-fulfilling one.

Have there been any predictions that met all these requirements? Abraham Lincoln's dream about his own murder seems to have been one example, and there may have been others, but they, too, would be of no interest to the adept of scientism because they do not fit into the canon. The number or frequency of such occurrences makes no difference, first because they cannot be planned, and secondly because their workings are in-explicable by the presuppositions that govern scientific inquiry. Nor can such experiences be converted into natural laws.

The reluctance to delve into these matters may be partly a fear of the risks involved in investigating the unknown: the risk, in particular, of being faced with the need to revise some of the most deeply rooted elements of the canon. There is also the risk, once an interest in these things is displayed, of falling victim to the tricks of some agile illusionist. There is no doubt that this is an area in which there is no lack of delusions, hallucinations, naivety and plain fraud; but whether or not there is any-thing else to it is not a question that should be simply dis-missed, for there is also no lack of phenomena that are clearly not the result of either fraud or delusion.

Direct experience of supernatural forces is something we must desire very strongly – why else would the world be full of people who once noticed a stain on a bit of rock that reminded them of the image of Christ or the Virgin Mary and since then have been rushing around spread-ing the good news to all who would listen? Occasionally such people may find a receptive ear, although not from the Church, which has recently displayed no eagerness to follow up, let alone attest, alleged miracles of this type. Superstitions abound in the world, and many of them are not worth investigating, except perhaps from a psychological or sociological standpoint. Some are dangerous; some are simply pathetic like the so-called cargo cult, immortalized in a film of Jacopetti. The history of witchcraft is not exactly encouraging, and yet today there are still people, mainly women, who think they have the ability to cast spells and bring misfortune on others by their magic. But the rationalist does not distinguish between superstitions which are worth investigating and those which are not. Witches do not generally advertise their powers to all and sundry, but if one were to succeed in finding out what spells a witch had cast on whom, and when, and if it then transpired that the victim did indeed suffer whatever misfortunes the spell was supposed to inflict, the rationalist would still put it down to coincidence, and no amount of successful spells would shake his refusal to credit the possibility of magic.

Since our reactions to events that are out of the ordinary depend upon certain doctrines and attitudes that we take as given, it is impossible to define superstition in such a way as would meet with universal approval. There are plenty of good reasons for supposing that, alongside the types of energy known to science and capable of being partially harnessed, there is another kind at work; and that there are certain talents and forms of communication which differ from the ordinary. Perhaps what is at work here is a kind of 'unknown guest', to borrow a title from Maeterlinck: some curious kind of energy which cannot be harnessed for systematic use in the way that electromagnetic waves, for example, can be harnessed, and which appears and disappears in sporadic and unexpected ways. The ability to exploit it may be given to all or only to a few; it may be constant or sporadic; but everything leads us to suppose that such energies and forms of communication do indeed exist. It is quite unrealistic, however, to imagine that they could ever be harnessed as an efficient and generally available technique, organized so as to give predictable results, or reduced, even theoretically, to phenomena that are already known. They are by their very nature ephemeral and impossible to organize in a systematic way; they seem to depend on some kind of force which appears and disappears according to their will. This is why expressions of belief in their existence will always provoke anger and outrage among those who, if they were to yield, would be forced to change their canon and their ideology.

It remains to consider whether belief in the existence of supernatural forces is on the whole a good or a harmful thing, regardless of the truth of the matter and independently of what such forces can or cannot bring about. There is a distinction to be made here. The burning of witches cannot be upheld as an example for us to follow, but it is no longer practised. Knocking on wood, on the other hand, is a harmless kind of superstition. If we believe that we are sometimes able to direct supernatural forces, the fact that we make use of this ability can be a good or a bad thing only insofar as our intentions are good or bad: if our intention is to harm others it is always bad, even if we do not succeed in our aims. As for the belief that there are supernatural forces which are favourable to us and to our worthy projects, that is surely a good thing, for it will reinforce our determination to accomplish those projects through our own, natural, powers.

18
ON NATIONAL
STEREOTYPES

It is a fact seldom noticed that a great deal of our mental universe – our image of the world and of other people, and our reactions to them – is made up of, or caused by, stereotypes. By stereotypes I mean those spontaneously arising quasi-empirical generalizations which, once established in our minds, are almost impossible to shift in the light of subsequent experience. This is a natural and perhaps on the whole beneficial arrangement: stereotypes – of things and people, nations and places – are indispensable to our mental security. This is why, whether they are plausible or half-true or simply false, they tend to survive disproof by experience – unless their effects are obviously harmful. If they are innocuous in their practical effects, they will persist despite the counter-examples thrown up by experience because we feel safer with them than without them: discarding them would impose on us a constant need for vigilance and consign us to a permanent state of mental uncertainty and disarray.

In this respect national stereotypes are no different from others. Take, for example, the stereotype of England as a rainy country. England's reputation for raininess is not based on any study of meteorological statistics, but on a spontaneous generalization. Once such a reputation has been established, it is maintained by a peculiar logical – or rather illogical – mechanism. When it rains in France, it just rains; each rainy day in England, however, is taken as confirmation of the stereotype that England is a rainy country. But the converse does not apply: a sunny day in England is logically irrelevant to the workings of this mechanism; it does not disturb the stereotype. Our normal, incurable, everyday thought processes do not and probably never will abide by sensible Popperian rules. We need stereotypes because we are, on balance, better off with them intact.

Each tribe or nation invariably produces stereotypes of its neighbours and of other, more or less familiar, tribes. Such stereotypes are often half-respectful and half-scornful. Thus we 'know', for example, that Germans are disciplined and humourless, that the English are reliable and narrow-minded, that Poles are courageous and disorganized, Jews clever and tactless, Americans friendly and naive, Czechs hard-working and mean, and so on. Examples are never lacking and counter-examples never count; the stereotypes are always safe. And if challenged, we have an infallible safety-net in such phrases as 'Oh yes, I know there are exceptions . . .', or 'Some of my best friends . . .'

The study of stereotypes is important, but not because it has the power to destroy them; rational arguments and statistics are probably helpless in the face of deeply in-grained images. Such images can change only if circum-stances demand that a different image be substituted. The extermination of the Jews by the Nazis, for example, cannot plausibly be accounted for by a previously exist-ing negative stereotype of the Jews. The Nazis certainly did their skilful and efficient best to exploit and reinforce that stereotype when the Germans found themselves in need of a scapegoat on which to hang the blame for their misery; but it was this misery and despair that made the Nazi programme of genocide acceptable.

National stereotypes do not necessarily carry the seeds of hatred. Some do and some don't. If they do, those seeds become a deadly weapon when other factors, in parti-cular war or the threat of war, come into play and con-ditions require it. Countries that have never been at war, or only for a short time, tend to form more benign stereo-types of each other – although even these are seldom entirely innocent or entirely positive.

The Jews, because they were present in almost all the European countries, were in a peculiarly privileged posi-tion: they were stereotyped everywhere. How the image of the Jew differed from place to place, according to local or historical circumstances, is a matter for a separate study. But the stereotype often – albeit not always – included, alongside the kind of unflattering descriptions that are fairly standard in tribal animosities, some horrifying and potentially deadly accusations – most strikingly that of ritual murder. Among peasants in particular there were some truly impressive and astonishing stories to be heard: at the age of ten I was told by another boy that the Jews cannot see the sun, and when I asked why in that case they wore sunglasses, I was told that they were only pretending. Incredible but true.

But leaving aside blood libel and similar horror stories and absurd superstitions, there is usually a grain of truth in the stereotyped pictures of foreign nations. Most often they are not just whimsical products of sheer fantasy, concocted *ex nihilo*, but rather simplified, petrified and inflated reflections of experience. There is, after all, such a thing as a historically shaped 'national character', and it is never composed solely of virtues. Although it obviously cannot be attributed to individuals ('every Pole is courageous and disorganized', 'every Jew is clever and tactless'), it does lend itself to rational study through an analysis of typical patterns of behaviour. And many nations have reflected some of their own less edifying qualities in literature, art and jokes: Jewish humour and Yiddish literature are an inexhaustible treasury of knowledge about the Jews' none-too-flattering perception of themselves, while the 'national vices' of the Poles have long been a favourite target for Polish writers and journalists.

The investigation of national stereotypes, a peculiar branch of social anthropology, can greatly contribute to our understanding of what 'national character' is – not because our stereotypes are an undistorted image of other nations and races, for that they certainly are not, but because in judging others we involuntarily reveal our own patterns of perception, and thus our own vices and virtues. In other words, stereotypes may well reveal more about the stereotyper than about the thing stereotyped. Thus while the investigation of stereotypes is unlikely to make them disappear, it may be of some practical benefit, for knowing how others see us gives us a better insight into ourselves, even if we think (as we usually do) that the way others see us is unjust. We can recognize ourselves in a distorted looking-glass (the best caricatures bear a strong resemblance to their originals); but the distortion itself, by exaggerating some of the features of the original, can also be useful, for it contributes to our understanding of ourselves.